RUNNING

with the

MIND of MEDITATION

RUNNING

with the

MIND of MEDITATION

Lessons for Training Body and Mind

||||||||||||||||||||||||||||||||||||||||||||

SAKYONG MIPHAM

HARMONY

BOOKS · NEW YORK

Published in the United States by Harmony Books, an imprint of the
Crown Publishing Group, a division of Random House LLC,
a Penguin Random House Company, New York.
www.crownpublishing.com

Harmony Books is a registered trademark, and the Circle colophon is a
trademark of Random House LLC.

Originally published in hardcover in the United States by
Harmony Books, an imprint of the Crown Publishing Group,
a division of Random House LLC, New York, in 2012, and
subsequently published in paperback by Three Rivers Press, an imprint
of the Crown Publishing Group, a division of Random House LLC,
New York, in 2012.

Grateful acknowledgment is made to Shambhala Media for permission
to reprint "Freedom" from *Snow Lion's Delight: 108 Poems* by
Sakyong Mipham. Copyright © 2005 by Sakyong Mipham.

Library of Congress Cataloging-in-Publication Data
Sakyong Mipham Rinpoche, 1962–
Running with the mind of meditation / Sakyong Mipham Rinpoche.
—1st ed.
p.   cm.
1. Meditation—Buddhism.   2. Spiritual life—Buddhism.
3. Running—Religious aspects—Buddhism.   I. Title.
BQ5612.S235 2012
294.3'4435—dc23   2011029751

ISBN 978-0-307-88817-4
eISBN 978-0-307-88818-1

Printed in the United States of America

Book design by Lauren Dong
Cover design by Jennifer O'Connor
Cover photograph © Philip and Karen Smith/Getty Images

5 7 9 10 8 6 4

First Paperback Edition

To the well-being of my wife, Khandro Tseyang,
and my daughter, Jetsun Drukmo

Contents

Victorious Vairotsana,
May your swift feet take us to enlightenment

Preface

Throughout my life, I have always enjoyed some sport. In my role as a spiritual leader and a Tibetan lama, I have been trained in horsemanship, archery, and sacred dance, as well as martial arts. I have always felt that some kind of physical activity was essential for well-being, as it gives a sense of confidence and enthusiasm.

It was only later in life that I took up running in a serious way. Running has been a real joy for me, an opportunity to be outdoors and to meet new people. It has benefited my health and well-being and has allowed me to offer something back to the world.

Meditation is something I have done throughout my whole life, and it is part of my cultural and spiritual heritage. Over the years, I have been asked on numerous occasions to put some thoughts down regarding the relationship between mind and body. Eventually I was asked to write a book on the topic of running and meditation. At that time, I felt I needed more experience as a runner, so I ran several marathons, which gave me some insight into the training process.

To me, the relationship between meditation and running is natural, for one is a training of the mind and one is a training of the body. However, I am hardly an expert on running. This book is therefore not a training manual, but a guide to integrating particular elements of meditation into the activity of running. I offer basic meditation instruction and explain those fundamental principles I have found helpful in running.

I also give pithy instructions and some themes that might be helpful in integrating running with the mind of meditation. Even though both activities can be complicated, I have kept the themes simple, trying to show where they overlap.

Meditation is an essential and integral part of my life, and combining the principles of meditation with running has been a delightful experience. I certainly hope the reader enjoys both activities, as I have.

Meditate with delight and run with joy. See you on the cushion or on the trails!

PART I

RUNNING

with the

MIND of MEDITATION

1
Running with the Mind of Meditation

We woke up early to sneak out of the monastery and get our morning run in before the ceremonies began. We drove to a nearby reservoir, got out, and began to stretch. It was only three thirty, and the early morning Indian mist and the coolness of the night still hung in the air. We were all a little nervous and excited, as we were running a new route.

We slid down an embankment, found the trailhead, and began to run, mostly at a slow jog—with the reservoir on one side and open grasslands bordering a teak forest on the other. Even though none of us had slept very much the night before, we felt very awake. As we ran through the grassy country-side, Josh Silberstein, my assistant, said to me, "Is there anything we should be watching out for, Rinpoche?" I quickly replied, "Yeah—cobras, leopards, wild elephants, and, oh, the occasional pack of wild dogs." Josh laughed and asked, "No, really, what should we be watching out for?" Looking at my face, he said, "Oh, you're not joking." "Not about that," I replied. At that moment, the nature of the run changed for him.

We ran through meterwide sinkholes and large mounds of dirt, which we soon realized were elephant tracks and dung piles. We came across wide-open expanses that reminded me of the African savanna. The trail then headed into the forest, lush and thick, part of what remains of the great teak forest that used to cover most of the subcontinent. Occasionally we would see someone walking along, carrying a basket.

The rhythmic movement of our feet created ease and relaxation in our bodies, revitalized by the fresh air. We remained alert and constantly aware of our environment, which helped us to be present in the moment. Even though we weren't saying much, there existed between us the camaraderie of an unspoken language, a deep feeling of appreciation that we were alive and healthy. We felt fortunate to be able to run. This was no ordinary run: we were training for the Boston Marathon, only two months away. Luckily we did not encounter too many wild animals while enjoying the Indian wilderness.

As the sun rose, we returned to Namdroling Monastery, in southern India, where I have spent much time meditating and studying Buddhist philosophy. On this stay, I was visiting my spiritual teacher, His Holiness Penor Rinpoche, to receive teachings and empowerments. *Rinpoche*, the Tibetan honorific for high lamas, means "precious jewel." In the Tibetan Buddhist tradition, before engaging on a spiritual path or beginning meditation, one needs to first receive authorization and transmission from a teacher. This keeps the spiritual lineage pure. In this case, I was receiving transmissions of the Mipham lineage. I am considered to be the rebirth of Tibet's Mipham the Great (1846–1912), one of the most revered teachers that Tibet has produced.

I have always found a natural relationship between running and meditation. Running can be a support for meditation, and meditation can be a support for running. Running is a natural form of exercise, for it is simply an extension of walking. When we run, we strengthen our heart, remove stagnant air, revitalize our nervous system, and increase our aerobic capacity. It helps us develop a positive attitude. It creates exertion and stamina and gives us a way to deal with pain. It helps us relax. For many of us, it offers a feeling of freedom. Likewise, meditation is a natural exercise of the mind—an opportunity to strengthen, reinvigorate, and cleanse. Through meditation we can connect with that long-forgotten goodness we all have. It is very powerful to feel that sense of goodness: having confidence and bravery in our innermost being.

Just as in running, in meditation we leave behind our daily concerns—the daydreaming, stress, and planning. We become very present. We enter into the now. By doing that, our mind builds strength. Our nervous system begins to relax. We develop appreciation and awareness. Our intelligence and memory become sharper. We are able to see the world from more than one perspective. We are no longer imprisoned by emotional highs and lows. Love, compassion, and other positive qualities become more easily accessible. Just as in running, when we finish meditating, we feel refreshed, and much for the same reason: meditation is a natural, healthy activity.

People sometimes say, "Running is my meditation." Even though I know what they mean, in reality, running is running and meditation is meditation. That's why they have different names. It would be just as inaccurate to say, "Meditation is my exercise." I have known some advanced meditators who have been able to bring their meditative mind—that strength and relaxation—into their body with its channels, nervous system, and muscles. They become strong, radiant, and resilient. We even have a type of meditation in Tibet called heat meditation, in which yogis who are able to use the power of their mind to control their body heat meditate in subzero conditions for months, wearing only a cotton shawl. However, it is unlikely that they would be able to run a sub-three-hour marathon.

Likewise, it is unlikely that we are going to attain enlightenment by running, even though some have tried. It is not a matter of choosing what is better—exercising the mind or exercising the body. Rather, these activities go hand in hand. We need to exercise both our body and our mind. The nature of the body is form and substance. The nature of the mind is consciousness. Because the body and mind are different by nature, what benefits them is different in nature as well. The body benefits from movement, and the mind benefits from stillness. When we give our mind and body what benefits them, a natural harmony and balance takes place. With this unified approach, we are happy, healthy, and wise.

Even in the ancient world, it was understood that people are happier when their minds are flexible and their bodies are strong. In the modern world, we are faced with conditions that challenge this mental and physical balance. We sleep less now, so we are often tired. We end up sitting down a great deal, riding in cars or buses in order to work in ill-designed chairs that give us back problems and bad circulation. The quality of the air in our environment may be poor, so we become even tighter and more tired.

Often we are stressed from the moment we wake up. The alarm clock goes off—hardly a substitute for the sun gently rising. E-mailing, texting, working on the computer, and watching television can be draining. Many of us rarely have full or complete conversations because we don't have time. Even our food is constantly being manipulated.

Both physically and mentally, we are taking on a great load. In order to handle that load, we need to attend to our well-being. Because the mind and the body are intimately connected, relieving the stress of the body through exercise has an immediate effect on the mind: the mind is no longer dealing with the discomfort of the body. If the body is relaxed and flexible, that is one less thing for the mind to think about. The physical act of running thus provides some mental relief, especially the greater the distance run.

In teaching my first meditation and running workshop, I was struck by the number of participants who were ultra-marathon runners. When I considered their experience, it made sense. After you run for a while, what do you find in there but your own mind? You work with that mind by meditating regularly.

Running works with the periphery or the superficial level of thoughts, concerns, and worries. Meditation not only deals with the periphery, it goes all the way down to the core. The path of meditation can be used in simple and immediate ways. It will help you recover from a stressful day or clear your mind before making an important decision. Or it can further your understanding of the nature of reality—all the way to enlightenment.

2
Building a Base

One of the most important people in my life as a runner is Misty Cech, an accomplished athlete and a well-known figure in the Boulder, Colorado, running community. I first met Misty in early 2003 when I was in Boulder promoting my book *Turning the Mind into an Ally*. Misty had been highly recommended as a trainer, so I contacted her for a run.

Upon our first meeting, Misty said, "It's such a beautiful day, why don't we try running outside?" At that time, I was accustomed to short runs on the treadmill. Since Boulder is at an altitude of more than five thousand feet, it is not the easiest place to begin running. We ran around the reservoir. Misty was bouncing along like a deer, while I was just trying to make it through the run. I felt more like a young puppy trying to keep up with its mother. Misty talked a lot and mentioned that she was honored to run with me. Meanwhile I was wondering if I was going to make it around the loop.

I could tell that Misty wanted to ask me something. Just as we started running up a big hill, she said, "Rinpoche, I have just one question. What's the difference between Buddha and Jesus?" I answered, "Do you think we could get up this hill first?" That was the beginning of a beautiful relationship.

After I'd been running for a while, Misty told me that I needed to think about "building my base." Jon Pratt, a fellow runner, had been encouraging me in the same direction. At that point, I was a little puzzled by this mantra. All I knew was that, whatever it meant, it involved a lot of running.

After several months of building my base, I began to understand what Jon and Misty were talking about. The base, as it turned out, was simply doing enough running, without overdoing it, to build the integrity of the bones and the strength of the tendons and muscles. This would slowly power up my basic physiology so it could handle the running. It was very similar to the first stages of meditation, in which we focus on building strength.

Curious about the process of building the base, I discussed it with my osteopath, Peter Goodman, whose understanding of the body is amazing. He also has a 3rd degree black belt in Tae Kwon Do, so I always joke with him that he could first break people and then fix them.

Peter said that the theory of building a base made sense to him. For one thing, the bones are not stagnant; they are constantly changing and developing. Because they have blood vessels running throughout, through the pressure of running, they become harder and more resilient. Likewise, the tendons become conditioned and tough, and the muscles become strong.

I was told that building a base would take about two years. That seemed like a long time; I wasn't even sure if I would be running by then. But, in fact, it did take about two years. During that time, my body was first getting used to running and then getting good at it. Building a base was a process of taking what I already had—my own lungs, muscles, bones, and tendons—training them to run, and gradually increasing their ability.

This process of taking the inherent structure of the body and strengthening it through regular and repeated runs is very similar to training and developing the mind in meditation. The Tibetan word for meditation is *gom*. It essentially means "getting used to, familiarizing." Meditation, then, is the act of familiarizing your mind with what you want it to do. That process of familiarity is just taking qualities and abilities that the mind naturally has, focusing on them in a methodical way, and thus building your base.

The bones and tendons of the mind are mindfulness and awareness. Mindfulness is the mind's strength, and awareness is its flexibility. Without these abilities, we cannot function. When we drink a glass of water, drive a car, or have a conversation, we are using mindfulness and awareness.

Unless we train it, the mind does the minimum necessary to fulfill a function. In that way, it is like the body. For example, our muscles and bones are strong enough for us to walk—but not to run, unless we have conditioned them. Without conditioning, even a sudden dash to keep our kids out of harm's way—or to catch a plane or a bus—will tire us out. Similarly, our mind has developed enough mindfulness and awareness to drive to work, but if we had to drive across the country, we might not have the stamina to stay on the road. Someone who makes long drives all the time, like a trucker, can do it much more easily.

The difference between the mind and the body is that no one is surprised to get winded while running to catch the bus. Nobody gets mad at themselves, saying, "I can't believe I can't run 26.2 miles!" However, when we become overwhelmed by longer hours at work, more e-mails, or more parenting duties, we become irritable, moody, and unhappy. It doesn't occur to us that our mind is out of shape. We put more stress on ourselves because we assume we should just be able to handle it all. We should not be surprised when we can't, for we have not built the base of the mind.

Because I was raised in a culture of meditation, meditating has always been natural and practical for me. My father, Chögyam Trungpa Rinpoche, was one of the greatest meditation masters that Tibet has ever produced. My mother was known as a gifted meditator even as a young girl there. I grew up with powerful, intelligent, and charismatic people who expounded the virtues of meditation and the need to take care of our mind. For me, meditation became as natural as drinking water or going for a walk. I grew up with proof that it works.

The West is not generally a culture of meditation, so of course many people here are unfamiliar with it. To some, it is quite mysterious. However, these days there is more exposure to meditation, and more people in the West are interested in it, especially as studies show its effectiveness in stress reduction.

When learning to meditate, it is important to have proper guidance and personal instruction. Posture, attitude, obstacles, and antidotes—all of these require good coaching. So I will try to present some basic facts and fictions of meditation to help you build your base.

As I mentioned earlier, movement is good for the body, and stillness is good for the mind. To lead a balanced life, we need to engage and be active, and to deepen and rest. When we are on the go—running, talking, working—the mind is engaged in a sympathetic nervous system process. If we don't balance the sympathetic with the parasympathetic nervous system process, in which we deepen and rest, we eventually become wired, edgy, and emotionally sensitive. Long periods of overstimulation—too much activity—begin to affect the organs and blood flow. Mentally we may become dull or jaded. Most important, we are not able to have deeper, more contemplative thoughts.

When we are active, we are generally engaged in tried and tested habits, and it's hard to change them when we're on the go. Often it takes some tragedy or major life shift to slow us down and pique our interest in cultivating a deeper parasympathetic mode. Keeping our body still and relaxing the mind while staying focused, as we do in meditation, is tremendously beneficial. But because we aren't accustomed to such a contemplative state, it may make us feel uncomfortable. We have difficulty changing our habits.

Meditation recognizes this difficulty, and that is what meditation is essentially addressing. In learning to meditate, we are first introduced to the technique of peaceful abiding, a period of stillness and deepening. When we feel comfortable with that technique, we train in deeper contemplation, in which we reflect on how we want to lead our life and begin to cultivate different mental habits. In meditation, we are creating new pathways for the mind, the brain, and even the heart. That's how we build a base.

In meditating, just as in running, we are engaging in something that is very different from what we've ever done before. So, especially in the beginning, we should not overdo it.

3
The Breath

Life is breath. Breath is life. According to the meditation texts, we breathe 21,600 times a day. That ability to breathe correlates directly with our life force energy. The breath circulates life force energy throughout our whole body. Over the period of our lifetime, this breath slowly decreases. What we do, how we live, what we eat, how we exercise, and what kind of relationships we have obviously affect our health, the breath, and therefore our life force energy. The health of the breath and how we manage our breath is an essential aspect of life.

The breath has a direct effect on the state of the mind. In fact, according to the Tibetan medical texts, abnormalities in the breath can lead to unstable mental states. We all know that the flow of oxygen and the oxygenation of the blood are directly linked to good health. Feeling slightly down and lethargic can result from a lack of good blood flow, and thus oxygen.

Paying attention to the breath as we exhale and inhale is extremely beneficial for the body and the mind. It helps to detoxify the mind from stress and negative thoughts and emotions, including regret. The breath is like the waves in the ocean that help circulate the water so that it does not become stagnant. Therefore when we pay attention to the breath, we are automatically brought into being present. This clarifies our mental state.

Generally our mental state becomes congested because we are thinking of the past or the future. If our mind is trapped in the past, it is pointing in a retrospective direction and feels sullen or gloomy. If we perceive the past to be the highlight of our life, subsequent events take on a depressed nature, since it appears that things are only getting worse. At other times, reflecting on the past too much brings about regret. We feel bad about something we did.

Conversely, if our mind is in the future, we might be stuck in a fantasy of hope that gives us a false sense of optimism and diminishes what we are currently doing. Excessive thinking about the future can also bring worry and anxiety because we do not know what might happen. Uncertainty brings uneasiness.

Of course, reflecting on the past can help us realize how we did something then and how, in the present moment, we could do it better. The future is important in terms of projecting forward our aspirations. But that leads us back to the present, because that is where we fulfill our aspirations.

Past events are already gone, and the future is yet to happen. It is only in the present that we can be in our life. The present is the joystick, controlling the moment, and thus the direction our life takes. Being with the breath is the most effective way of being in the present. It completely connects us with reality.

Being able to acknowledge the breath and then appreciate the breath, becoming intimately involved with the breathing process, is a key to meditation—and to running. The breath is like the green grass of the earth that we are standing on. We are often unaware of where we are standing. So in the beginning, most meditators have difficulty finding the breath and then appreciating it. We either get distracted by some thought, or we find relating to the breath to be boring.

The practice of meditation is the practice of developing

interest and appreciation in our breath. When we do this, we are showing interest in ourselves, our well-being, and our life-force energy. We are developing the ability to show interest in our own life and in what we are doing. That is why we feel the benefits of meditation immediately: we simply notice life more, pay attention to it more, and appreciate it more.

Initially, when meditation practitioners find their breath, it is shallow. As they become proficient in the technique, the quality of their breath deepens. The resulting strength and relaxation begin to pervade their whole body.

Similarly, when people begin to run, their breath is shallow. Beginning runners often even tend to hold their breath or to use only a portion of their lungs. When our breathing becomes hard and quick, we may be overwhelmed. We aren't familiar with rapid breathing because we've never experienced it before. As we begin to run more, we begin to relax with the breathing. This can be accomplished by breathing deeper.

After we become proficient runners, we realize that the human body is designed to breathe. In fact, much of our physiology is centered around the breathing. Our lungs take up our torso and back. The swinging of the arms and legs are pumps.

If we develop a relationship with our breathing, we do not have to struggle with it as much. Intuitively, runners know this. As we become more familiar with the process of breathing, we are essentially developing a relationship with the most elemental aspects of being alive. In meditation, placing our attention on the breathing takes the mind from daydreaming, worrying, thinking, and fantasizing. It gives our mind something healthy to do.

4
How to Meditate

When I was trained in meditation as a child, I was asked to sit there and follow my breath for an hour. I found my mind darting from one thought to another. The act of paying attention to the breathing and following it seemed quite arduous. In a very basic way, I was not in shape. My mind did not have the strength to hold what I was focusing on for more than a few moments. But after a short amount of practice, I was able to find my breath in minutes—and follow it.

Through my continued training, I have used a wide range of meditative techniques—from the simple stabilization of focusing the mind, to visualization, to contemplative meditation, to the use of mantras. All these depend on developing some basic aspects of mindfulness, which we could equate with strength training, and awareness, which we could equate with flexibility, endurance, and stamina.

In this chapter, I am going to offer instruction for one of the most basic and helpful meditative techniques. The process essentially consists of paying attention to the breathing. This is often called following the breath, or mindful breathing. It leads to peaceful abiding.

To train in this technique, first take the appropriate posture. Sit still, in an upright and comfortable way. Whether you are sitting on a cushion or on a chair, hold your spine upright, with a natural curve. Rest your hands on the thighs, with arms and shoulders relaxed. The chin is slightly tucked in, and the eyelids are relaxed. Relax your face and jaw. The tongue is also relaxed, the tip resting against your upper teeth. Your mouth is ever-so-slightly open. If you're sitting on a cushion, keep your ankles loosely crossed. If you're sitting on a chair, keep both feet firmly on the floor. Rest your gaze roughly six feet in front of you.

Now take your mind away from its current thought or worry and decisively place your attention on the breathing. This is known as placement, the first of nine stages in the process of strengthening and developing the mind. These are placement, continuous placement, repeated placement, close placement, taming, pacifying, thoroughly pacified, one-pointed, and equanimity. The first three stages are connected with stabilizing the mind.

Because we have not worked with the mind before, our first experience is that it is continually moving. The mind is perpetually flooded with thoughts. This stage is likened to a waterfall; the mind feels like a torrent of water.

Initially, it is important not to feel overwhelmed or disheartened by the influx of thoughts, simply recognizing just how many thoughts are coming into our mind. As we continuously and repeatedly place the attention back on the breathing, the mind becomes stronger and stronger. It's like doing repetitions in the weight room.

The breath itself is rhythmical, soft, consistent, and soothing. By meditating upon the breath, we are getting used to the breath. Through that familiarization, the mind is now absorbing positive and helpful qualities.

Next we follow one cycle of breathing. This is ordinary breathing; nothing is exaggerated. The breath leaves the lips and nostrils. It dissolves at about six feet in front. At the end of the breath, there is a slight pause, a slight openness. Then we begin to follow the breathing cycle back to the lips.

By placing the mind on the breath, we are practicing mindfulness. We are strengthening our mind, building the base. With this seemingly simple technique, our attention is becoming stronger. Plus we are not thinking about other things, so naturally there is peace, which is very helpful for the mind.

After you do this for a few cycles, you may lose your mindfulness and instead chase thoughts about what happened that day. So the next thing you practice is not being distracted by thoughts. This takes awareness. It does not really matter what kind of thoughts you are having. When you become aware that you are thinking, simply acknowledge that you are thinking and bring your attention back to your breath. You can say to yourself, "Not now, thoughts," or remind yourself, "Oh, I was thinking." Don't feel bad; just return to the breath as quickly and simply as you can. This is how to train in the stages of placement, continuous placement, and repeated placement.

Try to gently and firmly keep your mind on the breathing. When you are aware that you are thinking, remind yourself to come back to the breath. Taking your attention away from thoughts and placing it on the breath is the focus of meditation, which in this simple form is simply the process of being mindful of the breathing, being aware that you are thinking, and returning your attention to the breath.

As we continuously and repeatedly reassociate the mind with the breathing, we are creating stability. This fourth stage—being able to keep the mind on the breath without distraction—is called "close placement." Our meditation is stable, and our mind is slowly being tamed. This is how we establish a base in meditation training. When we've established the ability to pay attention to the breath, our ability to focus on any other object or endeavor is strengthened.

When you begin to meditate, try to do twenty to thirty minutes of meditation at each session. If your mind is not used to meditating and these longer periods are difficult, shorter sessions might be helpful. Even ten minutes can be beneficial, especially if repeated several times throughout the day. For example, you could meditate for ten to fifteen minutes upon waking, ten to fifteen minutes before lunch, ten to fifteen minutes in the afternoon, and ten to fifteen minutes in the evening.

Even if you are meditating for only ten or twenty minutes per day, it is helpful. As in running, frequency helps to build the base. Later you'll find that thirty minutes go by quickly and easily, and you'll soon be meditating for forty-five minutes to an hour. Later still, you'll be able to do several hours in a row.

When you sit down to meditate, setting a timer can be useful. Obviously it is not good to keep checking your watch, as you might discover that you have supernatural powers that can slow down the time. Traditionally, meditators use incense, not only as a scent offering—and the smell helps to keep them awake—but also as a timing device. Most incense sticks last about forty minutes, and the sticks can be broken in two.

It is also good to clearly mark the beginning and end of a session. By doing this, you acknowledge that you are making the space in which to work with your mind. Traditionally a small bell or gong is used, but you could also begin and end the session by doing a warrior bow: place your hands on your thighs and bow your head and torso forward. You should avoid being completely without structure, with no beginning or end to the sessions. This laissez-faire attitude begins to diminish the power of the meditation session, and it begins to yield fewer results. This is a bit like hanging out in a gym without working out.

In meditation, a general sense of decorum, appreciation, and cleanliness is helpful. If you are disheveled and the room is a mess, it is challenging to develop precision of mind. At the same time, these sessions should have a level of ease, relaxation, and comfort so they do not become too uptight and too rigid. Stretching the legs every forty minutes and moving slightly can help. Wiggling your feet and ankles can help with circulation and reduce the chance of the legs falling asleep.

If you find yourself in a great deal of pain sitting on a meditation cushion, you might want to sit on a thicker cushion or move to a thicker chair. You may want to integrate brief periods of walking meditation with the sitting. I describe this in chapter 18. You might also consider getting bodywork or doing more stretching.

In Zen monasteries, drowsy meditators are hit on the shoulder with a piece of flat wood. In Tibetan monasteries, round sticks or small whips are used. This keeps everyone attentive. However, if we are practicing by ourselves, we need to be our own disciplinarians, for we could do anything we like and no one else would know. We thus should have a balance of structure and relaxation on the outside, and mindfulness and awareness on the inside. This keeps the meditation both warm and crisp.

5
Taming the Horse

One of the great meditation masters of Tibet, Khenpo Gangshar, was a tutor to my father. Khenpo was a brilliant scholar. As a precocious young man, he received a unique blend of practical and analytical education, like some of the great philosophers of the Hellenic period. He wrote several meditation texts.

In one of the meditation texts, he asks, "Which is most important, the body, speech, or the mind?" Then he examines all the pros and cons of each. With the body, we feel hot and cold. We experience great pleasure and pain. We are able to dance, meditate, and enjoy delicious food. With speech, we can sing, talk, and communicate. With a few simple words, we are married, and with a few other words, we could start a war. With the mind, we can have thoughts and ideas, gain knowledge, and conceive of the past and the future. The mind can imagine places that it has never been.

Khenpo Gangshar eventually concluded that even though the body, speech, and the mind are all important, the mind is the most important. The mind is the king or, in more modern terms, the boss. Only with the mind can we initiate movement in the body and sounds in speech. The more capable that mind is, the more profound effect it will have. So we must take care of the mind.

In the meditation tradition, the mind is considered to be located in the head, the heart, and throughout the body. However, mind and body are ultimately a single entity. This is the feeling of unity, oneness, or centeredness. In particular, there is said to be a unique relationship between the breath and the mind. In Tibet, we say that the breath is like a horse, and the mind is like the rider. When the breath is calm and in control, it is much easier to access the mind. The Tibetan word for breath, or wind, is *lung*. This wind represents movement and energy throughout the body.

A heightened thought process such as worry increases the movement of wind. The more erratic the wind, the more it moves throughout the body. We experience it as agitated, discursive thinking and emotional highs and lows, which translate into stress—blocked energy. When we run, that wind begins to settle down, and the blockages begin to clear.

In Tibet, we have a traditional image, the windhorse, which represents a balanced relationship between the wind and the mind. The horse represents wind and movement. On its saddle rides a precious jewel. That jewel is our mind.

A jewel is a stone that is clear and reflects light. There is a solid, earthly element to it. You can pick it up in your hand, and at the same time you can see through it. These qualities represent the mind: it is both tangible and translucent. The mind is capable of the highest wisdom. It can experience love and compassion, as well as anger. It can understand history, philosophy, and mathematics—and also remember what's on the grocery list. The mind is truly like a wish-fulfilling jewel.

With an untrained mind, the thought process is said to be like a wild and blind horse: erratic and out of control. We experience the mind as moving all the time—suddenly darting off, thinking about one thing and another, being happy, being sad.

If we haven't trained our mind, the wild horse takes us wherever it wants to go. It's not carrying a jewel on its back—it's carrying an impaired rider. The horse itself is crazy, so it is quite a bizarre scene. By observing our own mind in meditation, we can see this dynamic at work.

Especially in the beginning stages of meditation, we find it extremely challenging to control our mind. Even if we wish to control it, we have very little power to do so, like the infirm rider. We want to focus on the breathing, but the mind keeps darting off unexpectedly. That is the wild horse. The process of meditation is taming the horse so that it is in our control, while making the mind an expert rider.

It is common to imagine that in meditation we are not supposed to think. That is somewhat inaccurate. What is really happening in meditation is that we are developing the ability to think when we want to, and to not think when we don't want to. We're developing the ability to direct our thoughts and focus them on the object of our choosing. For example, if we want to develop compassion, we practice focusing on thoughts of compassion, or on thoughts of people who move us toward compassion. If instead we find ourselves thinking about ice cream, and then about how our mother used to bake cookies, we are back on the wild horse. We did not intend to think those thoughts. When the mind is running everywhere, it is less available, and we feel tired, heavy, and stressed.

It's true that in the beginning stages of meditation, we want to avoid too much thinking. At that point, thinking just stimulates the wind, which we experience as discursiveness. Therefore the way to train the horse at every stage is to bring the mind back to what we want to focus on. In the beginning, we want to focus on the breathing.

By following the breath and beginning to pace the breath,

we develop a steady, rhythmical flow, out and in. This flow calms the mind, which is like training the horse. Every time the horse wants to leave the trail because it sees some nice morsel of grass—be it a random discursive thought or a large fantasy—we bring the horse back to the trail. In this case, the trail is the breath.

6
Peaceful Abiding and Contemplation

nitially, following the meditation technique is like taking kids to school: our mind might be kicking and screaming that it does not want to go. We experience this as many thoughts and emotions arising as we return our mind to the breath. However, with the right motivation and good technique—placement, repeated placement, continuous placement, and close placement—we are gentle and firm, and our mind shows up for class every day.

Once our mind is tamed, we enter the stages of pacifying and completely pacifying. We begin to abide peacefully. In Tibetan, this is known as *shiné*. Some people know it by its Sanskrit name, *shamatha*. Learning to abide peacefully is the reason that people engage in meditation at all. We are training ourselves to reduce stress. With the simple act of placing the mind on the breathing and staying there, we develop a level of peace because our practice is one-pointed. At the one-pointed stage, our mind is no longer distracted. At the next stage—equanimity—our mind is strong, stable, clear, and joyous.

I find that teaching meditation to people who run is sometimes easier than teaching it to those who don't, because runners have a natural feeling for the breath. For runners, working with the breathing is straightforward. Even though this is true, it is difficult to establish peaceful abiding when we are running.

Why? In order to access the mind, the wild horse has to be tamed. That comes through the constant application of the meditation technique. Even though there are some mental benefits in running, they are usually achieved not by taming the horse, but by exhausting the horse. By moving, we are physically exhausting the wind. Afterward, we feel calmer because the wind is more settled. Thus the mind is more present and at peace. So the clarity and peace of mind we feel after running is mostly because the wild horse is tired, not necessarily because it has been tamed. The mental clarity brought about by physical exercise is temporary. When the horse has more energy, it resumes running around. Then we have to go for another run, exhausting the mind again. Using running as a way to train the mind is incidental, whereas the peace and clarity that come from meditation are cumulative.

Generally speaking, knowledge in the mind builds upon itself. We can learn the letter *A* today, the letters *B* and *C* tomorrow, and eventually we learn the alphabet. Then we can create words and sentences and, after that, write books. The strength of the body, however, has to be constantly maintained. Relatively speaking, of course, the body can build fitness in itself, and the mind can forget knowledge. But, generally, the body's benefits through exercise are temporary, while meditation allows for a cumulative benefit to occur.

Ideally, our daily routine will include both exercise and meditation. Mind training can help athletes get more out of their physical training. It helps them to be undistracted and focused so they are not having negative thoughts during competitions. At the same time, it allows them to develop the skill of being gentle and firm with themselves. For meditators—or anyone pursuing knowledge—exercise helps keep the body from becoming a nuisance. When we're not feeling pain or discomfort, our intellectual work takes less effort. Ultimately, both the mind and the body are things we should cherish. The body is the magical horse, and the mind is the magical jewel.

The power of peaceful abiding meditation should not be underestimated on the basis of its being the first technique we learn. It might lead us to experience light, clarity, or joy. These are not alternate universes, but the innate qualities of a healthy mind.

When we are able to stabilize our mind with peaceful abiding, we advance to another kind of meditation based on developing insight. In Tibetan, it is known as *lhakthong;* in Sanskrit, *vipashyana.* These words mean "clear seeing" or "superior insight." With this kind of insight we sharpen our innate intelligence, or *prajna.* This second kind of meditation is a more advanced meditation. It is essentially the process of educating the mind so that it draws the right conclusions. To do this we use a conceptual framework. In other words, we use our sense of duality—subject and object, here and there, this and that—to investigate the truth about reality by contemplating that truth. By seeing the truth as separate from ourselves, we engender a way to experience it. True reality is beyond concept, beyond the duality of this and that.

In contemplative meditation, rather than continually placing our mind on the breath, we place it on certain powerful themes, such as generosity. As our mind becomes more familiar with them, those themes begin to make an imprint. This technique works with two principles, that of the word and that of the meaning. For example, we may decide to contemplate the theme of love. The more we place our mind on that word, the more it engenders that feeling.

As we run, we have various thoughts in our mind, so if our

focus is well trained, we can direct it to certain themes. For example, we could focus on feeling fortunate or grateful. With enough familiarity, that contemplative meditation becomes our attitude.

Often when I run, I try to generate the theme of benefiting others. Although I may not necessarily be benefiting others as I run, afterward I find myself helping others more easily. If we contemplate feeling fortunate, we might find ourselves feeling more appreciative afterward, or if we have been contemplating love, kindness and compassion might arise more naturally. Even though running is not meditation per se, we do spend much of the time hanging out in our mind, and after we've strengthened our focus, we can use it in this way. Parts II–VI of this book contain some contemplations to try while running. However, we start by practicing contemplative meditation while we're sitting down.

Practiced properly, this second kind of meditation leads to the discovery of wisdom, which we define as "nonconceptual understanding." It is transcendent knowledge, a level of consciousness beyond using concept to understand things. Wisdom transcends duality. The constructs of "this" and "that" dissolve. This is what we call enlightenment, in which our knowledge goes beyond the three times of past, present, and future.

Thus we can use meditation simply as a tool to stabilize and strengthen the mind, achieving a level of peace, or we can use it as a tool to develop wisdom. Even if we want to develop wisdom, we have to start with stabilizing and strengthening. It is hard to be wise, calm, or peaceful if our wild horse of a mind is galloping around and the rider is flailing here and there. That's why it is so important to have formal periods of sitting meditation, in which we work on taming the horse and making the rider more capable.

7
Difficulty in the Beginning

n running and in meditation, the beginning can be the most challenging time. It can be difficult because we are attempting to change our habits. In running, we're trying to change our physical habits, and in meditation, we're attempting to change our mental habits. In both cases, we need to be very clear in deciding that it's what we want to do.

The beginning of running is a fragile time. We are tight, we don't have much stamina, and we tire easily. Determination and exertion are essential. We are taking our body from being sedentary to being active. Our tiredness and tightness reflect the difficulty of that transition as we increase our heart rate and blood circulation.

This early phase is critical. If we overdo it, the exercise is too intense and we stop. If we don't apply ourselves enough, we never quite develop the habit. What I often recommend in the beginning is "walk running"—walking interspersed with brief bouts of running. This gentle and integrated approach seems to work well for beginners. Running does not become overwhelming, and at the same time, the short bursts of running allow the heart rate to rise and the blood to flow. Even ultramarathoners use this technique of walking and running.

In fact, when I introduced running to my wife, Khandro Tseyang, I encouraged her to mostly walk, with two minutes of occasional running. I was wary about giving her too much instruction, as it is often delicate and challenging to coach one's spouse. After several months, my wife was able to run twenty to thirty minutes. Later, to celebrate our wedding anniversary, we went for an hour-long run together. I was extremely proud of her progress, which had occurred because she didn't overdo it.

In the beginning, like many runners, I found the first twenty minutes or so the hardest part of running. I thought, "I'm just not in shape." So it seemed natural that I would feel a level of discomfort. Sometimes I felt like I wasn't going to be able to run more than a few minutes. My legs would feel heavy, disconnected from the body. Later, when I was in much better shape, I still had a period of slight discomfort at the beginning of a run. I realized this has nothing to do with being in shape or out of shape. It is just the body and nervous system switching from being sedentary to being active.

Even now, if I stop running for a few days and then start up again, I feel like I've lost a lot of my fitness. When I told this to my trainer, Misty Cech, she replied, "Rinpoche, I don't think you've lost any fitness in the last few days. It's just that the nerves in the body have to be awakened again." I have found this to be quite true.

Conversely, in meditation, the initial phase can be challenging for the opposite reason: we are slowing down. When we first sit down and begin to meditate, the mind has been very busy. It's been speeding around, and now we are encouraging it to move more slowly by focusing on the breath. In the beginning, we might feel impatient and agitated, but this has more to do with our mind not being comfortable with the new speed limit than it does with the practice of meditation itself.

In the beginning of running and of meditation, one of the biggest obstacles is laziness. One kind of laziness is basic slothfulness, in which we are unable to extract ourselves from the television or couch. In this case, just a little bit of exercise can send a message to the body that it is time to move forward. Even putting on workout clothes and beginning to stretch helps bring us out of our sloth. By the same token, sitting down to follow the breath for even five minutes has the power to move us out of laziness. Another form of laziness is that we don't make time in our busy, speedy life to go for a run or to sit down and practice.

Another obstacle at the beginning, particularly in meditation, is forgetting the instruction. Even though we have gotten ourselves to the meditation seat, we forget to apply the technique. We were instructed to focus on the breathing and release thoughts. However, instead of following these instructions, we are either just spacing out or just thinking away. This is like putting on our running shoes, shorts, and T-shirt—and just standing there.

Although the process of meditating is different from running, the tools are the same: we need to be determined and exert ourselves. If we can get through the beginning, we will probably be successful. Obviously we will have challenges throughout our journey, but at the beginning of both activities, perspective and perseverance lead to big rewards.

In the beginning, it is important not to overdo either activity. We all overdo it occasionally when enthusiasm gets the best of us. For example, I was in eastern India in the state of Orissa, engaged in a four-month ceremony. The rituals started at five in the morning and lasted until eight thirty or nine at night at the Ripa monastery, seat of an important Tibetan Buddhist lineage that is headed by my wife's family. Her brother, Jigme Rinpoche, a prominent lama and community leader, was my host. He knows that I like to exercise.

When I arrived, Jigme Rinpoche told me that he had a surprise for me. When I got to my quarters, I was astonished to see a treadmill. I'm not sure how he got it there, but I sure was happy to see it. I was certain that I would make good use of it over the next few months.

The only time I could run was either very early in the morning or late at night, and the heat and humidity of India never seemed to ease. The treadmill was in a very tight space. This was compounded by random power outages, as the community gets some of its electricity from freestanding generators.

I developed a good routine of scheduled runs on the treadmill, but I usually kept them under an hour. About three weeks into my stay at the monastery, I thought it would be good to do a long run on the treadmill. So I ran for about an hour and twenty-five minutes. In order to do this, I had to start at three in the morning. To make matters worse, I was on malaria medication and only getting from four to five hours of sleep a night. I finished the run at about four thirty. I felt a little tired, but I was fine.

The only problem was that I now had a sixteen-hour day in front of me. These ceremonies can become very complicated with chanting and ritual movements. In addition, I was sitting on a throne in the front of the room, visible to everyone in the very large audience.

By the end of the day, I began to feel tired and lightheaded. I had clearly overdone it. So for a while, I backed off from running and focused on stretching. I kept using the treadmill for the duration of my stay, but I did not run for that long on the treadmill again.

Of course, we all go through our own experiences. If we do not push ourselves enough, we do not grow, but if we push ourselves too much, we regress. What is enough will change, depending on where we are and what we are doing. In that sense, the present moment is always some kind of beginning.

8
Motivation

Running and meditation are very personal activities. Therefore they are lonely. This loneliness is one of their best qualities because it strengthens our incentive to motivate ourselves. The Tibetan word for motivation, *kunlong*, means "to rise up." It is literally that aspect of our mind that rises to the occasion. That moment of inspiration—when we know what we are doing and why—is like an arrow that we shoot. Wherever that arrow goes, our mental and physical troops will follow.

When I teach people to meditate, I ask them to contemplate their motivation, for I feel that the moment we discern our motivation is essential to whatever we do. The contemplation is simple: "What am I doing? Why am I doing it?" Even discovering that we are not sure what our motivation is, or finding that we do not have motivation, is a very telling sign. Whether we are meditating for ten minutes or ten days, motivation is an essential ingredient.

The same applies to running. With a single moment of good motivation, we are able to rouse ourselves, get through the door, and run six miles. Conversely, with a diminished motivation, we may find it hard to get out of bed.

When I first began running, eight miles seemed like a long run. When my trainer, Misty Cech, and marathoner Jon Pratt suggested that I run a marathon, I felt intimidated. At that point I was not even sure how far a marathon was. Like many, to me the word *marathon* meant "an extremely long way." I got tired just imagining it. My motivation had not risen to the occasion.

The moment that I thought, "I can do this," however, my motivation allowed me to shoot my mental arrow 26.2 miles, and I began my training in earnest. Within weeks, my mind had become accustomed to the idea of running a marathon, and I signed up for my first—the Toronto Waterfront.

One of the tools we learn from meditation is developing this ability to raise the appropriate amount of motivation. We learn to watch our mind and to pay attention to what makes our mind motivated, what feeds that motivation, and what sustains it.

There may be people in our lives who motivate us, or we may be motivated by a movie or television show. For example, seeing *Chariots of Fire* made me immediately want to go for a run. I was similarly inspired by watching *Without Limits*, the story of Steve Prefontaine, who had so much heart. Although it's fairly easy to find sources of outside inspiration, ultimately it is best to generate our own motivation. In this way, we are not always waiting for the next pep talk.

The whole premise of motivation is that there is no limit to it. In the meditation tradition, we talk about three kinds of motivation: small, medium, and large. Rousing small motivation is contemplating that the meditation practice is helpful for ourselves: we can develop a good attitude, which helps alleviate our mental and physical suffering. Medium motivation is realizing that we can use meditation to discover the nature of reality, what lies underneath all our discursiveness and habitual patterns. Great motivation is that we can attain enlightenment and therefore help all beings. The exercise of rousing motivation is not about what is possible or impossible, but rather about seeing how far we can expand. When we contemplate our motivation, we expand our attitude from being concerned with just ourselves to caring for the whole world.

You can apply this small, medium, and large motivation to running as well as meditation. Pacing is important. For example, if you have no motivation at all, then immediately expanding to a large motivation might be too big a leap. So to apply motivation skillfully, start with the small. If you are tired and don't want to run, telling yourself that you should run ten miles might just make you more tired. But with a smaller motivation, you might convince yourself that a twenty-minute run would be possible. Then when you go outside and run for only twenty minutes, you will feel satisfied. And after only twenty minutes, you might find yourself doing thirty or forty.

Motivation is not about trying to trick yourself. It's a way to expand your mind, raising its horizon. Each run should have a view. There may be times when you need to challenge yourself with a greater level of motivation. For example, you may have only been doing ten miles, so you challenge yourself with the motivation to run for twelve or fifteen. Even if you make it only one mile farther, your motivation has put you forward.

Similarly, you might challenge yourself with the motivation to meditate for thirty minutes instead of fifteen. Or you can rouse the motivation to pay closer attention to the technique. Remember why you are meditating: to balance the activity of your life by working with your mind. Motivation is not simply about getting yourself to the meditation seat.

Paying attention to your level of motivation helps in daily life, too. If your motivation when you get up in the morning is to have very little contact with anyone, come home, and go to bed as soon as you can, almost everything that occurs during the day will make you feel brittle and irritable, because it's in your way. The space afforded by a slightly larger motivation—the motivation to use the day to appreciate being alive, for example—allows for so much more to happen. Articulating and expanding your motivation when you wake up in the morning has the power to change your whole day.

In addition to small, medium, and large motivation, there is short-term and long-term motivation. If you are to achieve great things, you must have some kind of long-term motivation. Without the long-term motivation, the short-term motivation might become monotonous. For example, if your long-term motivation were to make it to the Olympics, this driving theme in your life would put all of your training into a larger perspective. From that long-term motivation would come your short-term motivation: you'd be devoted to training daily and raising the bar on a regular basis.

On the other hand, if you have long-term motivation without short-term motivation, you might become overwhelmed, because you don't have a way to move toward the longer-range plan. Then you lose sight of your long-term motivation. When that happens, your runs or your meditations become less frequent. They may begin to feel pointless or overwhelming. It's essential to keep balancing these two types of motivation.

We always have a motivation. If our motivation to run or to meditate becomes weaker, then the motivation for sitting and watching television becomes stronger. That is called "negative motivation," which is really the opposite of motivation: instead of rising, the mind is collapsing within itself. When we feel overwhelmed or unmotivated, we aren't returning to a neutral state of mind. Rather, our mind is sinking. This is not necessarily depression; it is the mind finding reasons for why it cannot do something—as opposed to why it can. When our mind sinks like this, we have talked ourselves out of something instead of into something. Meditating helps us see these shifts in our mental attitude. After a while, we can see them in our running, too.

The success of both running and meditation lies in the ability to handle our motivation. The point of handling our motivation is not necessarily to channel it into a drive to be successful; that would be ambition. Rather, the point is to allow ourselves to see what is possible.

When I finished my first marathon, along with thousands of others who had trained hard to be there, part of the joy lay in experiencing the fulfillment of our motivation. With appropriate motivation, we are naturally successful. That is what brought all those smiles on race day. With suitable motivation, we are all winners.

9
Marathon

My main objective in running my first marathon, the Toronto Waterfront, was simply to finish. On a cold and gray morning, I was accompanied by the ever-cheerful Misty Cech, my trainer; Jon Pratt, a seasoned marathoner; and Nick Trautz, a professional cross-country skier. We had all been training over the summer, so there was an air of anticipation.

People seemed amazed that a Tibetan lama would be running a marathon. Members of the Toronto Shambhala Centre and the local Tibetan Buddhist community had volunteered to support the race, handing us water and energy gel along the way. Many of these individuals had not been to a race before either, so it was a day of firsts, with lots of curiosity and excitement.

As we waited for the start, stretching and jogging in the cold, I decided to put on some new socks, ignoring the adage "No new equipment on race day." Unfortunately I would soon understand what this meant. But since I was inexperienced and new to racing, I thought that a new pair of socks would be good for my first marathon.

We entered the starting area. The gun fired. At first there was not much movement, as we were in the pack, but then there was a shuffle, and we took off. I was nervous, for on this day I would run farther than I had in my whole life. As a runner, my strategy was to not go out too fast. As a meditator, my strategy was to remain present and relaxed throughout the course. Many runners dashed past us.

We made our way through the streets of Toronto, running with thousands of people. After about a mile, someone on a bicycle yelled out, "Only twenty-five more to go!" which was not too comforting. I ran well for the first few miles, but soon I noticed that my socks were rubbing. Around mile six, I started to get a blister. Misty asked how I was feeling. Apart from the blister, I felt good, but I knew it could threaten my race.

Soon I could feel that the blister had grown to cover the ball of my left foot and was inching down to the midsection. My foot throbbed with pain. When Jon asked me how I was feeling, I knew he would only worry if I mentioned the blister, so I said I was fine.

I knew from my meditation training that I could not let the pain steal my mind. Therefore I paid attention to the feeling of pain, but I did not let it dominate my mental space. This was a delicate balance: I didn't want to ignore the pain, so I stayed with it, and at the same time, I could not allow it to preoccupy me. Instead I focused on my good fortune to be in good enough shape that I could run a marathon. I appreciated the brisk day and my running companions.

About twelve miles into the race, I knew I needed to make a decision. If I were going to continue running, I would have to pop the blister. In a queasy moment that I did not share, I stamped my foot down hard until I felt the blister pop. Then I just focused on finishing the run.

The majority of the race was on Yonge Street, one of the longest streets in North America, which takes you into downtown

Toronto. As I turned a corner, I saw a man on a bike who was yelling at runners as they passed. I wondered if he might be crazy, but in fact he was one of the "psychs on bikes," there to offer encouragement. He shouted, "This is the moment you've been training for!" I thought, "He's right." After the long hours of training and with only a few miles left to run, I was determined to finish well. I increased my speed, and in those last miles we passed those runners who had gone out too fast in the beginning and were now slowing down. Our moderate beginning was paying off.

We came into downtown with thousands of fans screaming. The last few miles seemed so long because people kept calling, "You're almost finished!" which was not really true. Finally we saw the finish line. Our bodies were completely exhausted, but we were smiling as we crossed. Everyone in our group had made it. I received my medal for finishing the race. There were people sticking bananas and water bottles into my hands. I headed over to where our fans and friends were waiting. Everybody was extremely cheerful and amazed that we had done it. That's when I started limping.

My physician, Mitchell Levy, was there and eager to see how I was doing. When I told him I had a blister on my foot, he said, "That's not bad, considering you just ran a marathon." But when he saw it, he yelled, "Oh my god!" With better bedside manners, he would have said, "That doesn't look too bad," but in fact, it didn't look good. The blister ran along the bottom of my foot for about four and a half inches. My sock and shoe were completely bloody. The other runners were shocked. They said that they wished that I had told them, but there would not have been any point. It was a dramatic end to a dramatic day.

We returned to the hotel, washed up, and had a celebratory dinner. As we were heading to the restaurant, a few blocks away, our hostess, Tara Slone, asked, "Sir, would you like to walk or drive?" I turned to her, smiling, and said, "What do you think?"

10
Tiger, Lion, Garuda, Dragon

began to run simply as a way to get some exercise. Soon enough, however, I found myself applying certain principles I have learned in a lifetime of meditating. This evolved into breaking my training into four phases: tiger, lion, garuda, and dragon. In the Shambhala tradition of warriorship, these creatures are called the "four dignities." They represent the inner development of a courageous individual. The idea is to develop balance and integrity. The result is strong windhorse, *lungta*—the ability to bring about long life, good health, success, and happiness.

Shambhala was an ancient country in central Asia where rulers and citizens attained a deep level of enlightenment. It is said that the entire society was founded on the premise of humanity's inherent basic goodness.

The Shambhala teachings present goodness as our base and splendidness as our natural state of being. These qualities are neither spiritual nor worldly but inherent—there to be uncovered. Over the centuries, the teachings of Shambhala have been passed on. I am the inheritor and holder of these teachings, which are characterized by the notion of bravery. One engages in life courageously, but without aggression. The Shambhala path is thus a path of warriorship.

This process of warriorship begins with the tiger, which is

the principle of mindfulness, which leads to contentment. This is the phase in which we work on technique, on paying close attention. It's when we build up the base. In the tiger stage, we learn how to focus. At the same time, we practice not overdoing it, so that we simultaneously develop gentleness. In short, by applying mindfulness and focus, we accept and appreciate who we are.

The Shambhala teachings say that the tiger is friendly to himself and merciful to others. In the context of meditation, this means that we accept ourselves and appreciate others. In relation to running, being friendly to ourselves means being kind to our running mind. Being merciful means being merciful to our body.

What makes the tiger powerful is that it completely embodies confidence. The tiger is not disheveled and mindless, tripping over logs and breaking branches. Rather, it moves with grace and power, the result of having full command over its own being. This is the principle of embodiment. In addition, the tiger is extremely careful, in the best sense of the word. I find this a good way to describe the beginning phase of running, when we are just learning which clothing is appropriate, how to hold our posture, and how much or how little to run. Rather than brashly overdoing it, we are somewhat careful as we monitor the development of precision and strength.

The next phase is the lion, which is associated with joy. In Tibet, the snow lion is pictured leaping about in Himalayan wildflower meadows, full of exuberance as it enjoys fresh mountain air. In the Shambhala teachings, this phase of training is connected with the joy that good conduct brings. The lion shows the power of virtue: compassion and kindness are stronger than selfishness and aggression.

Therefore we say that the lion is perky. We worked hard

as a tiger, so now we enjoy our fitness and the freedom that it brings. We have built a strong base, and we know how to run, so we can throw away our watch and head out the door. With less concern about how many miles we run or how fast our intervals are, we enjoy nature, the streets, and being alive.

The next phase is the garuda—a mythical eaglelike bird that has two arms as well as wings. When the garuda hatches, it is instantly able to fly in any direction, surveying everything below. Traditionally, the image represents the inconceivable power and awesomeness of the mind. That's why the garuda is said to be outrageous—not in the reckless sense, but in the awesome sense. When meditators enter the garuda phase, they are no longer trying to figure out how to meditate; they have mastered the technique and gone beyond the reference point of hope and fear. For runners, this outrageous phase of training means that we are competent and accomplished. Now we can challenge ourselves. This may lead to some outrageous runs.

The last of these four phases is represented by the dragon. The dragon flies in the sky, always appearing with the clouds, creating a mysterious effect. In Asian culture, this is not a creature to be feared and slain. Rather, the dragon represents wisdom, intelligence, foresight, and omniscience. In the dragon phase of our running, we are basing our activity on intelligence and compassion. We are no longer running for ourselves, but to benefit others. Extending ourselves, we join with others to run for a charity or a cause, like world peace.

These dignities are progressive, in that one leads to another. At the same time, they are all-inclusive. In the lion, garuda, or dragon phases, one never leaves the tiger behind, as all of these concepts are interdependent. In this light, elements of the dragon are in the tiger. Each phase emphasizes a certain aspect.

As I run, I find that applying the principles of tiger, lion, garuda, and dragon gives my training variety, interest, and enjoyment. I've also felt great satisfaction as I accomplish the different phases. Most important, applying these principles has allowed me to use running to benefit others. I can share the joy I feel while running with the rest of the world. As you'll see in the following chapters, there are many long- and short-term ways to use these simple principles—both in running and in meditation. They represent the development of the mind and heart from the beginning, all the way to full enlightenment.

PART II

TIGER

11
Mindfulness

One of the key elements of running with the mind of meditation is respecting your mind and your body. In the tiger phase, we focus on being mindful—of our breath, posture, thoughts, feelings, and the attitude we bring to our activity.

In both meditating and running, the tiger phase shows you things about yourself that you never noticed before. You get an intimate look at your own mind—its strengths and weaknesses. The tiger is refreshing in its humbleness and honesty.

When I first began to meditate, I was asked to pay close attention to how my breath felt: its texture, the feeling of it leaving my mouth and nostrils, the time it took to exhale, how it felt to inhale. With these simple instructions, I developed the rudimentary skill of mindfulness: just being present for a simple single action.

How difficult can it be to pay attention to the breathing? In the beginning, it is quite challenging. As you follow the breath, you are distracted by your senses—by the smell of coffee brewing or the sound of a bus. These distractions stimulate thoughts, and your mind tends to chase them. In that moment, you lose your focus on what you intended to do: keep your mind on the breath. When the mind darts from what it sees to what it hears to what it thinks, that is distraction—the thief of mindfulness.

With mindfulness, we are training our ability to focus on an object and stay with it. We are exercising a muscle of the mind. The more we exercise our mindfulness, the stronger it becomes. In the beginning, we are like a child at the gym: we can only hold the two-pound dumbbells for a few seconds. Our mind is distracted, and we drop the weight. In weight training, we keep exerting ourselves and increasing the weight; it is natural and choiceless that our body gets stronger. Similarly, in meditation, the mind will get stronger if we keep exercising our mindfulness.

During this phase of the tiger, the best advice that I received was to be gentle. We are not taking up running with the mind of meditation to give ourselves a hard time. A Shambhala slogan associated with the tiger is "Friendly to yourself." A good friend has our best intentions in mind. Friends don't yell at us, "You're a lousy meditator!" or "You can't run!" They encourage us, reminding us why we got into running or meditation in the first place. They help us stick with it. Most important, a friend wants us to do what is best for our progress. Therefore being friendly to yourself means offering yourself a little leeway, honesty, and humor. A combination of mindfulness and friendliness is ideal.

When we start to meditate, at first we are able to stay with the breath for thirty seconds, then forty-five seconds, and then a minute and a half. With gentleness, we keep reminding ourselves that we are building strength. Our mind is slowly getting stronger and, therefore, more mindful. This mindfulness is helpful for performing any task because our sense perceptions are sharper, our memory and focus are keener, and we are able to be more fully present for others.

An even bigger benefit of developing mindfulness is stability: we are training our mind to stick with its intention. We are using mindfulness like a kite string to keep our mind from following the winds of thought—whether positive or negative. With the stability that mindfulness brings, our mind is less frantic and worried. When people say that meditation makes them calm, they are often referring to this stability of mind. A stable mind creates the foundation for a happier and more contented person.

Mindfulness brings contentment and satisfaction. We need nothing but what we have, like a tiger preening. The tiger is very present. When we are very present, we project more health and power. We feel mentally at ease: quite simply, we are happier. This is why people continue to meditate—it brings a basic feeling of healthiness. In this healthy state, the mind is more likely to generate positive thoughts and, therefore, positive actions. Many of these positive thoughts are in fact already just below the surface of the mind.

If we are unable to stay focused in meditation, we cannot stay mindful, so we just become lazy and give up. Since we are not friendly to ourselves, we give ourselves a hard time, and the whole experience becomes painful. Or perhaps we become fascinated by our mindfulness, immersed in the pleasure of it. We become attached, which distracts us from the present moment. Mindfulness in itself is a fairly neutral action of the mind. You can use it to hold to anything. When you cannot do it, it is not mindfulness giving you a hard time; rather, the culprit is the reaction you had to straying from the focus.

Mindfulness does not care whether you stay with the object or not. So you should be gentle when you have strayed from the breath—or whatever you are using as your object of focus. Beginning meditators often become either harsh or laissez faire when they recognize they are no longer present. One should therefore be gentle but firm with what has just occurred.

Overreacting to a lack of mindfulness instigates discursive thinking. Gentleness is the key.

If we do not pursue mindfulness, earnestly stabilizing our mind in meditation, we will inevitably never feel the results. Therefore we might feel disheartened and give up. Our mind darting here and there actually weighs on us physically. We look nervous and strung out, more like a frightened deer than a tiger in its prime. Fortunately it is always possible to reapply ourselves with mindfulness, being gentle, friendly, and firm by reminding ourselves of the benefits.

The tiger phase is where we begin to build our character as a meditator and as a runner. We see clearly how focused or unfocused we are. We begin to see how many thoughts we have, and it is often surprising how random, bizarre, and even how negative some of those thoughts are. Although we may be able to run, we can no longer run from ourselves, because we've discovered how it feels to be mindful. This understanding is essential for success on the cushion and the trail. In later chapters, we will explore how mindfulness can be used in running.

12
Posture

During the tiger phase, we work on developing the strength and focus of our mind. With mindfulness and gentleness, the mind develops the ability to know what it is doing. Just simple attention to our running form is extremely helpful, so we focus on the posture.

This part of your training consists of looking at your posture, making sure that your body is aligned. Just like the meditation posture, your running posture needs balance and symmetry. If you don't run symmetrically, you can create unnatural angles that put more pressure on one joint or another. This can result in injury.

Often through bad posture while sitting and walking, due to chairs that are at the wrong angle or from slouching, you create tight muscles and an uneven tension in the body, so your running posture may be off-balance and out of alignment in the beginning. Paying attention to it now is how you ingrain the habit of good running posture. This mindfulness may also give you better posture after your run.

Running has many possible distractions, so you won't be able to focus continuously on your posture. You may have to avoid oncoming traffic, glance down at your watch, or drink from your water bottle. The point of the tiger phase is spending a higher percentage of your run focusing on your form.

If you find your mind wandering away from your posture, bring your mind back to it with every breath. You may become distracted and forget to do this, but when you wake up—just do it. On a forty-five-minute run, remembering to bring the mind back to your posture for even fifteen minutes is beneficial for the body and the mind.

There are a variety of techniques that emphasize different postures in running. I have tried a number of them, but I always come back to the technique I've found helpful in meditation: feeling the connectivity from my navel up through my central core, leading to my mouth and nostrils. Relaxing my eyes as I run, I drop my general focus from being in my head to being more in my core. I let my eyes see, my ears hear, and my nose smell without actively focusing on them, whereas in cooking, I would be paying special attention to those senses.

I keep a slight forward pelvic tilt in my hips, which allows the curve in my back to be natural. I try to maintain an upright posture, emphasizing my head and shoulders. I try to remember that my lungs are not just in the front of my body but are also in the back. An upright posture allows for the best and most efficient usage of the cardiovascular system. In meditation, hunching with a curved back not only creates physical pain further down the road, it also tends to generate more thinking.

Because we see running primarily as a movement in the legs, many beginners do not hold their torso in an upright posture. Collapsing forward puts pressure on the lungs and forces the head to go forward, adding extra weight in the front, throwing you off balance. It also creates unnecessary pressure in the spine and contorts the internal organs. Like meditation, running is a unique combination of relaxation, good posture, and symmetry. When we pay attention to our posture and apply some discipline to how we hold our body, joy and freshness arise. Good posture brings good meditation and good running.

Often beginners think that raising the legs extra high will make them run faster. However, running well has to do with knowing the result you will get from a particular effort. When I run, I try to lift my legs just high enough to create a more efficient stride. That means as little movement of the legs as possible. Of course, if I am sprinting, I may take a different approach for a different result.

As you run and feel the placement of your feet on the ground, pay attention to how you are landing. Are you landing on the heel of your foot, the midsection, or the ball? If you are overly supinating or pronating, with mindfulness you can begin to balance that tendency.

One day Peter Goodman, my osteopath, said, "Through the power of your meditation, you have retrained yourself to land at a better angle." While running, I had tended to supinate, but I was now able to land more in the center of my foot. This did not happen accidentally. It came through paying attention. Of course, we all have natural tendencies and our bodies are all different. In that light, there may not be a perfect running form, but rather one that is best for you.

I make a conscious effort to land on the front pad of my foot, just below the second toe. When I do this, I feel the line of pressure through the midsection of my foot, through my shin, up through my thigh, and through my hip joint. I try to relax my hips and remember that the psoas muscle between the spine behind the sternum and the inner thigh initiates the lifting of the leg, and that this muscle actually begins at the spine, behind and below the sternum. So I visualize the legs starting directly below the sternum, in the upper part of the torso and back, for that is where these hip flexor muscles that initiate leg movement begin. Seeing it this way helps integrate the lower and upper parts of the body. Then I relax my arms and hands, allowing them to swing naturally. With the movement of running or walking integrated throughout the whole body, the body will be in fluid motion, like grass blowing in the wind.

If we are too focused on other aspects of our life, we may not pay attention to our running. Thus our running may lack engagement, and with less focus, we may trip or fall. So before beginning a run, I determine my destination or the amount of time I might run. Within that basic parameter, I try to relax, consciously letting go of any other activities, plans, or concerns. This is an essential part of enjoying the run and its benefits.

Another technique you can use in the tiger phase is counting your breaths as you run. Find a quiet place, and, resting your gaze a comfortable distance in front of you—about fifteen to twenty feet—pay attention to every inhale and exhale that you take. Each full breath could take ten steps, assuming you are not sprinting. This practice should be done at a leisurely pace, on a surface that is not too heavily trafficked and that has good footing.

Count up to ten breaths, and then return to one. In this way, you could continue up to one hundred breaths. If you find yourself drifting off into fantasies, come back to the posture. Look at where you are and feel the ground under your feet. Look at the trail, the sidewalk, and the trees. Then, when you come back, begin to pay attention to the breathing: resume your tiger training. With these exercises, find a nice balance of not focusing too intently. Otherwise you might trip or not see a car. Conversely, if you are too loose with the technique, you will find yourself drifting into thought.

Other tiger runs could be going for a run without a headset or, if you are at the gym, not reading a magazine or watching television. Or, if you are used to running with friends and you usually talk, enjoy your run in silence. Pay attention to the elements instead. If it is cold, feel the cold. If it is hot, feel the heat.

If you are used to running with a headset and you begin to notice discomfort in your body, this might be a good opportunity to take off the headset and work with your mind. Recognize that a lot of pain is mental and try not to panic. Breathe deeply into the pain and relax. If you need to stretch, stop and do some stretching. Slow your pace. At times like these, it helps to remind yourself of the benefits of running. Try to inspire yourself. When negative thoughts come into your mind, try substituting positive ones.

13
Feelings

n beginning meditation, people often experience physical difficulties. Most of these feelings come from not being accustomed to sitting still for an extended period of time. After the initial period of settling in, there may be slight tension in the back or the knees. Aches and pains might arise. You could also find yourself feeling itchy, or irritated in other minor ways.

This phase is known as the mindfulness of feeling. It is a natural stage in the evolution of our practice. The majority of these irritations are mental. We have begun to settle into our body, and our mind begins to notice subtle variations in how we feel. Most of these minor irritations should be left alone. The mind will naturally begin to relax. If it becomes excessively irritated, you should shift, move, or scratch. Over time you will be able to gauge what to do. But if we are imaginative and practical, we can find different ways of continuing our meditation practice without physical difficulties infringing on its success.

Similarly, as we begin to run, we will notice different feelings. Some runners find these feelings disconcerting and try to avoid paying attention to them. This is understandable because the feelings are sometimes uncomfortable. But a majority of these discomforts are essentially the mind beginning to notice things about the body. Generally these aches and pains are superficial. We are feeling the mind noticing, more than the body hurting. So pay attention to these various feelings, because a big part of mindfulness is just noticing how you feel. Let the stiffness or aches and pains be your focus. By acknowledging them, you do not have to run away from them. Feeling the little discomforts is actually an important psychological step in being present. You may have felt tight all day, but now as you run you are totally aware of it. This mindfulness is a sign of a more discerning level of consciousness in which you are able to notice each thought and feeling.

By paying attention to how your mind and body feel, you are empowering both yourself and your running. Developing this respect for mind and body changes running from simple exercise to a journey of discovery and growth. Respecting how you feel during your run allows you to appreciate who you are in the very life you are leading.

Such mindfulness is not just a cerebral occurrence: staying mindful of how you feel instead of trying to distract your mind has its effect on the body, too. Mindfulness of body begins to stimulate your oxygen flow, the nervous system, and the various channels running throughout your body. Thus this level of mindfulness naturally gives you more energy, strength, and vitality.

The body may start off by feeling rather tight and sluggish. Later in the run, it may become fluid and strong. Then the body will feel tired. Paying attention to these phases not only keeps the running contemplative in that we continue to discover ourselves, it also keeps the experience interesting, which helps us to grow. Through modern science, we know that our consciousness is not just in the brain; it runs throughout the body. So by paying attention to your body, you are paying attention to your mind and therefore to who you are.

Injuries bring up many feelings, and being injured never comes at a convenient time. Often it happens when it is least expected. The first few moments after an injury are important. As soon as possible, we should acknowledge that we are hurt. Recognizing our injury is not a defeat, but rather shows courage. If we ignore an injury, recovery could take longer.

Often if we are in the middle of intensive training, we might also get angry or upset. Here, patience could be our best friend.

At the same time, we should not let injury become an excuse not to do some form of exercise, such as swimming or other forms of cross-training. Keeping the body active helps in the recovery, but if we are avid runners, keeping still can be more of a challenge. Without patience, people try to run again too soon and complicate their injury. Waiting out an injury is an excellent time to work on our meditation. I have found rehab to be a practice in itself, determining day to day how we feel and responding with the appropriate action—which may mean keeping still. We can use the time recovering from an injury to train our mind in gentleness and firmness.

In the tiger training, results arise from being friendly to ourselves and mindful of our body. As our body becomes more powerful and full, this approach is manifesting physically. When we run, we have more charisma and dignity. Athletes who have good mindfulness of their body exude power and strength as a result. Their tiger element is showing. This is where one athlete might intimidate another with physical prowess. Less confident athletes' minds are busy with distracting thoughts, so there is less power in their physical embodiment.

Embodiment takes place when the mind completely fills the body and they are synchronized. It is the feeling of being full and alive. This feeling is rich and powerful. When it is happening, we know it. But more important, we feel it. The mind and body are not disconnected, out of sync, or at odds. At a physiological level, our muscles are more full, and we feel more present and powerful. Like a tiger in its prime, we feel awesome. Conversely, when our mind leaves our body, we're like a balloon that has lost its air. We feel limpid and weak. When we are not embodied, we are very vulnerable to discursiveness.

Therefore when our mind is embodied in our physical activity, mindfulness is simply a natural outcome. Being present and undistracted is easy. This tiger phase is teaching us the principle of embodiment. In Tibet, we call this embodiment *lungta,* or windhorse. Windhorse is power that stems from egolessness. This level of mindfulness is not an inflated ego, but rather a human being who is being mindful—not distracted—and embodied.

14
Full-Heartedness

Being mindful is not simply keeping one foot in front of the other and watching the trail, it is also the attitude we bring to our run—full-heartedness and appreciation. If we avoid our mind and feelings while we run and then try to apply some mindfulness, we may experience a momentary benefit. But without enthusiastic engagement in what we are doing, a few mindfulness techniques are not going to help us use the mind of meditation in our run.

Mindfulness consists of noticing—being inquisitive and interested. Our mind is therefore full of whatever we are engaged in. This is opposed to half full or a quarter full. In that case, we are not being mindful. In running, lack of mindfulness results in tripping on the trail. In meditation, it results in getting distracted by a thought.

At the tiger level, mindfulness means full engagement with our running. We see the very act of running as a demonstration of who we are. The more we regard what we do as meaningful, the more meaningful it becomes. Whether the run is long or short, a full-hearted attitude brings satisfaction, enthusiasm, and vitality.

This principle of full-heartedness derails many potential runners and athletes. Because they consider the body secondary to the mind or regard their physical activity as a minor hobby or an obligation, they are mentally halfhearted. When they finally get to the act of running, there is only a quarter of their mind present to manage 100 percent of their body.

I learned a vital lesson when I began meditation: if I did not respect what I was doing, nobody else would. Meditation has further demonstrated to me that once you begin to respect yourself and what you do—not in an egocentric way, but with appreciation and self-worth—then any activity becomes meaningful. Life is to be respected, appreciated, and lived fully—instead of chastised or rushed through.

I aspire for full engagement even when I use the treadmill. Because I travel so much, I have spent a lot of time on a treadmill. I have run on treadmills that look more like torture devices than treadmills—no frills, just the belt, hard and uncomfortable. In certain developing countries, I've been on treadmills that don't even run on electricity. I've also been on treadmills that recognize the runner by a key you insert and that allows you to preprogram your run. Once I was running and there was someone on the treadmill next to me who stopped running to answer a question I asked and flew off the back of the treadmill. Being fully engaged has many benefits.

I have also had nerve-racking runs in Nepal, where because of the unstable government, the electricity was being rationed. So I would be running on a treadmill, and it would suddenly stop. At other times, I would run on the treadmill, and everyone in the house would know because the lights would start dimming, since each house was allotted only a certain amount of voltage.

One of the things that I have learned over the years is that, approached the right way, the treadmill can be an excellent support and companion for training. While I was training for the Napa Valley Marathon, I would even bow before getting on the treadmill. It was a playful gesture of competition, and part of being fully engaged.

Often I see people putting on earphones and zoning out, trying to either numb their mind or distract themselves until their body is done running. Of course, I cannot be too critical of this technique, as some runners get into incredible shape this way. Music can be motivating. It can invigorate us, bringing our mind in tune with our body. In this way, music makes a powerful and inspiring tool. At the same time, music can be used as a way of disguising our workout—taking our attention far away from what we are doing. In this case, music becomes a source of distraction. So while at times music can seem helpful, ultimately it challenges our ability to be present and embodied.

My approach is to make the treadmill run as interesting as I can. Given that none of us has ever gotten anywhere running on a treadmill, we can still imagine. I find that doing short intervals, surges, inclines—five minutes here or two minutes there—keeps the mind engaged, and the body gets the benefit.

In the modern culture of speed, we seem to not do anything fully. We are half watching television and half using the computer; we are driving while talking on the phone; we have a hard time having even one conversation; when we sit down to eat, we are reading a newspaper and watching television, and even when we watch television, we are flipping through channels. This quality of speed gives life a superficial feeling: we never experience anything fully. We engage ourselves in these activities in order to live a full life, but being speedy and distracted, we have never discovered what *full* means.

Since our technological era provides endless things to do, there is no end to how distracted we can become. Not experiencing things fully, we bear the brunt of this hysterical lifestyle. We get indigestion from eating too fast, we get into a fender bender from talking on the phone, or we have to split up from our partner because we have not been communicating fully.

Meditation is not just a simple technique for stabilizing the mind; it is also the discovery of how to engage fully, even while sitting still. It can definitely be applied to running, one of our liveliest activities. But if we engage in these two activities half-heartedly, simply trying to keep ourselves distracted all the way through, the lesson will be lost on us, and we will miss yet another precious opportunity to be present in our lives.

When we are running—and when we are exercising in general—we are engaged in one of the most intimate and meaningful acts that might occur during the day. Running full-heartedly turns a period of exercise into something that is healthy for the body and also for the mind. In this regard, being mindful brings life.

15
Running with Realities

always tell people that a successful meditation practice is one that you can sustain. It is not necessarily how long you can meditate, or how still you can be, if you just give it up the next day. First you must come to the conclusion that the activity is important. Then you should make it a daily occurrence, in which every day you motivate yourself in a different way.

Like meditation, successful running—or some form of exercise—is maintained throughout our life. The ability to do this comes from having the right attitude. What often derails this process is having a hot-and-cold approach, in which we train intensively and then give it up. The tiger incorporates meditation and running as a natural part of the daily routine, for these endeavors can bring health of body and mind only if we are consistent in practicing them.

When I travel to Asia, the flights are often fifteen to eighteen hours long. I try to stretch, move, and exercise. On one flight, I was able to do some mild calisthenics while everyone else slept. After about twenty minutes, the flight attendant approached. I assumed she was going to ask me to go back to my seat. Instead, she looked at me and said, "I really need to start working out."

Exercising regularly is challenging because we may get sick, or perhaps we need to focus on a large project. We may go into a slight athletic depression in which the thought of exercising is slipping farther and farther away. Even though I have remained fairly active throughout my life, I know very well what it feels like to be aerobically out of shape. When we become so sedentary that our body is almost addicted to not being in shape, getting in shape can be a challenging, painful, and difficult endeavor. The exertion it takes to get back in shape when we are out of shape is arguably more than it takes to stay in shape, for the amount of mental and physical stress is substantial. It may even feel like it is too late.

But fundamentally, the body wants to be healthy. It is naturally designed to survive, and it will quickly adapt to getting back in shape once we return to our routine. In the meantime, we may have to change the parameters about what exercise means. Even putting on workout clothes and beginning to stretch is a way to begin. Walking or jogging for five, ten, or fifteen minutes can be incredibly beneficial. Just this little bit of exercise sends a message to the body that it is time to move forward and improve.

When I was deep in my studies, I was engaged in Buddhist philosophy and metaphysics. The entire course ran for nine years, but I could never think about it in terms of one block of time—that would have been too overwhelming. Rather, I would break it up into years, months, and days. Even now, when I am teaching or involved in a meditation retreat, I try to keep my exertion very present by breaking things into small portions. In this way, what I am currently doing stays interesting, and the weight of the overall endeavor does not become too oppressive.

I also find it important to have some kind of plan for the workout that I am going to do, even if it is a plan to have no plan. Just jumping on the treadmill day after day with no strategy can get you into a rut.

Likewise, try to keep the goal of your tiger run very immediate. Approach it with a sense of general appreciation, and then find small objectives like a tree, a house, or the top of a hill to run to. Having arrived at a particular spot gives a feeling of satisfaction. After a while, these small achievements build up. Your willpower and ability strengthen. If you have made it so far, you will most likely make it the rest of the way. Similarly, if the situation is reversed and you have a series of small misfortunes, by the end of the day you feel tired and discouraged. These small moments do matter: they do begin to affect our state of mind.

One of the best tools for the continuity of training is gentleness. It doesn't help to chastise yourself for not running. At the same time, you need to be firm so you don't hurt yourself with lack of healthy activity. The wise are balanced, and the foolish are extreme. We all go through periods when we are foolish, and at times we are wise. But if we want longevity for our running, we have to be wise.

Being wise means doing what is good for you. That may not necessarily consist of following the best training method. Try to find a good balance between being too uptight and too lethargic. Even in the Western approach, too much sleep is worse than not enough. The feeling of vitality comes through good circulation and the consumption of food and water, and exercise increases both.

Often the sluggish feeling we experience at the beginning of exercise is due not only to the stagnation of the muscles, but to the stagnation of the organs. According to the Chinese system of medicine, stagnation is the cause of many illnesses. We can often attribute the feeling of sluggishness to the liver, which has over one hundred types of metabolism and is considered to be the "general" of the organs.

Eating and drinking late at night tells the liver that it needs to keep working. Therefore we sleep poorly and wake up sluggish. The liver becomes tired and has to work overtime. Not exercising compounds the stagnation because all the toxins are processed more slowly. The system is overloaded, which contributes to our heavy feeling. Only twenty or thirty minutes of exercise is often enough to move things along. Even if we are mildly sick, movement is helpful. It does not have to be a full-on run.

In a similar vein, if we have toxified our mind through too much television or arguing, meditation gives us a period of time to cleanse the mind, allowing us to reprioritize what is important and resetting our emotions.

Because I travel a lot, it is hard for me to follow training programs that are laid out in books, so I've had to adjust my program to my travel. You learn as you go. For example, generally you do not want to train too hard after a flight, as the body is swollen. To maintain my training I am constantly making microadjustments and running with realities. Even if you don't travel much, there is often some scenario happening that interferes with your running. First you are busy, then you catch a cold, and then the weather is bad.

It's not necessarily a problem to frequently adjust our running routine. It can be enjoyable because it keeps things interesting. Conversely, there have been times when I have been in a deep meditation retreat and I have had to wake up extra early to get some form of physical exercise. Even in those scenarios, minor alterations in the schedule keep things interesting. Obstacles do not have to be insurmountable, for our running and meditative character is being forged by these challenges.

16
Just Do It—with Gentleness

Sports often carry an aggressive edge, as reflected in Nike's "Just do it" slogan. I have seen the same advice in ancient meditation texts. My father often told his students, "Just do it!" It is not necessarily an instruction to be pushy or aggressive. Sometimes we need to just do it. The question then becomes, How do you do it?

My meditation teachers taught me that with aggression, you may accomplish some things, but with gentleness, you can accomplish all things. The word *gentleness* has many meanings. In the meditation tradition, it is associated with wisdom and power because it is considered the antidote to aggression. Gentleness is like water—it will eventually reach its goal. Aggression is like fire—it is quick and then it is gone. Since 70 percent of our body is water, we naturally have a lot of gentleness.

People consider aggression to be a positive aspect of sports. They might say, "You need to be more aggressive," which essentially means being more determined. Surely some coaches would like to peel away the raw aggression and just use the determination, for in order to be determined, you do not need to be aggressive. Those aggressive mental states are taxing. They impair our judgment. We are more emotional, so we are less able to observe reality accurately. We misread others' words or facial expressions, so we are less likely to understand things.

Even though most of us will inevitably find occasion to get angry or upset, it is not the best plan of attack.

Generally, when athletes are at their highest level of performance, they are in a gentle and relaxed mode of being that allows them to have awareness and perspective. Therefore, if we want to just do it, maybe once, aggression might seem necessary. We take "just do it" to mean "just push on through," and in pushing through, we may hurt ourselves. If we want to do it again and again, applying gentleness allows us longevity and success.

Aggression is a short-term solution for a long-term problem. Gentleness is persistent. Gentleness is therefore a sign of strength, while aggression is often a sign of weakness. Aggression is often a last resort. Where do you go from there? If you become more aggressive, you seem insane, whereas if you have gentleness, you are like a great ocean holding a lot of power.

Applying gentleness to running keeps our mind from becoming totally critical or getting into other extreme states. Gentleness allows us to keep our eye on the prize without getting infatuated and without losing heart.

With gentleness, we feel like we can run forever. With aggression, we feel like we can only dash to the next corner. With gentleness, we take a long run in stride. With aggression, we are concerned that if this run does not work, we might fail.

With gentleness, we no longer struggle with ourselves. When we are not struggling with ourselves, we are doing our best. We cannot do more than that. In fact, being gentle with ourselves, we may be surprised by how much we can do. We become inspired by our potential.

On the other hand, aggression is often the result of personal discontentment. We are not getting along with ourselves, and because of that inner conflict, we lash out at others. This kind of aggression thus comes from a lack of friendliness with one-self. To be gentle is to encourage ourselves. Since gentleness has a level of intelligence, we can clearly see our bad habits. Those bad habits are approached more straightforwardly when we can see them clearly. Gentleness allows us to have more skill and more options in how we overcome negative habits and ingrain positive ones.

Gentleness can be developed with simple thoughts. First, appreciate who you are and make friends with yourself. Look at what you can do, and don't allow what you cannot do to oppress you. Rather, regard it as a future adventure. The practice of meditation allows for this development to take place.

As I've applied the technique of gentleness while running marathons, it has allowed me to realize that I *had* trained for the race and that I was completely capable of doing it. I was kind to myself, being present with the pain and the joy, not flooding my mind with endless scenarios of what could go wrong. Gentleness allowed me to accept unforeseen obstacles. It kept me from talking to myself about not finishing. Gentleness thus became a matter of maintaining confidence while not being too self-engrossed and, at the same time, not objectifying the race. If I objectify the race, it becomes my opponent. If I simply run the race full-heartedly with gentleness, it becomes my ally. Gentleness allows us to utilize all the aspects of what is happening in the environment and to build a positive base around it.

To be gentle is to understand that life is a journey deserving constant attentiveness. Therefore it is gentleness that allows us to finish a marathon, not putting pressure on ourselves to immediately think about the next one. Gentleness is "just doing it" in such a way that we can do it again and again.

17
Taking on More without the Worry

People have different ways of dealing with stress—eating, drinking, exercise, and now meditation. Meditation, surely one of the first stress relievers, is based upon the principle of knowing what the mind can handle and what it cannot and then increasing its ability to handle more.

Meditation is also based on not having too many activities. Each of us has a natural amount we are able to handle. There is usually some tipping point at which the load shifts from being manageable to unmanageable, on both the macro level and the micro level.

The macro level pertains to our whole life cycle. Generally, the stress level increases as we get older, simply because we add more activities to our life—school, relationship, work, family. The micro level is day to day. Even in a very stressful period of our life, some days will be less stressful than others. In a less stressful period of our life, there will still be stressful days.

For all the technological advances of our age, our ability to deal with stress has not necessarily improved. Even though these technologies are supposed to help us, they often create stress with all their additional information and faster communication. The increase of speed and news brings the increase of worry—and more worry brings more stress.

We have two ways of accumulating stress: physical and

mental. Meditation can play a major role in reducing our mental stress. However, by strengthening the mind in meditation, we are not necessarily training it to handle more worry. We are increasing its strength and flexibility to handle more *without* the worrying. How much more? Infinitely more, according to meditation texts. I have met meditators who were jailed, tortured, beaten, and starved for many years. They said the key to their survival was meditating on limitless love and compassion. Nelson Mandela also forgave his captors in prison. Of course, we may not all regard ourselves as saints, but certainly with these examples, we too can expand our minds with these limitless qualities.

Meditation is not just a chamber in which miraculously our stress dissolves. Rather, it is like exercise. If we are curling weights to build our arms, on the way up, the tension in our arms is strengthening. On the way down, we can relax. Then we can do another curl. In the same way, meditation is both intensifying and relaxing. We strengthen our mind by coming back to the breath, and we relax by letting thoughts go. A key principle in stress reduction is the ability to let certain things go.

As I have said, the mind gets used to certain states—among them, worrying and stressing. According to Tibetan medicine, negative thoughts affect our nervous system and thus our muscles and organs. There is clearly a relationship between a healthy mind and a healthy body, and a relationship between imbalance and illness. We embody our worries. When stress is the basic state of mind, even good things stress us out. We have to learn to let go. Meditation gives us this training. Also, through running and the movement of oxygen, those internal stresses are unblocked, moved, and cleaned. That's how running helps reduce stress.

Generally, with more stress there is less happiness. Conversely, if we have fewer activities, we are less stressed, but this does not necessarily lead to more happiness. Most often our happiness comes from human interaction. Therefore it comes down to love and kindness, friends and family. Happiness is not necessarily how many things we have—happiness is the ability to share what we have with others.

18
Walking and Yoga

Even though there is a big difference between walking and running, many of the principles I have mentioned also apply to walking, probably the best of all exercises. It is low-impact, promotes circulation, and helps clear the mind. We should all enjoy a good walk, incorporating the qualities of mindfulness and gentleness.

Walking is traditionally used as a meditative discipline because it is slow enough that one can easily focus. It is often used to break up periods of sitting. The walking meditation I describe here is also a walking yoga, with the right hand placed over the left fist just beneath the solar plexus. The technique consists of walking slowly and gently, taking short steps, and focusing on the placement of one foot heel to toe, the shifting of the weight, and then the placement of the other foot. There is a feeling of balance and harmony with the movement of the legs and feet as you bring mindfulness to your body. This walking meditation is a way to integrate the mind and body by slowing the mind down. It creates an excellent bridge between meditation and running.

In Tibet and other parts of the world, taking long walks as a pilgrimage from one sacred spot to another is considered a path to great spiritual merit. Propelled by the right motivation and attitude, these long walks can become a way to cleanse the body of negative karma and engender the mind with virtue. I have gone on walking pilgrimages to various holy sites, walking all day long. Such walks provide excellent exercise while also enriching the mind. I also enjoy going on treks and hikes.

My wife and I often go for walks together. In fact, I may run faster than she does, but she is a much better walker. It is a wonderful way to be with each other. We do not necessarily need to talk. Walking can be a way of clearing one's mind as well as contemplating.

For me, practicing yoga has provided an excellent balance to running. Running can tend to tighten up the hips and the legs. Yoga loosens them. Yoga also provides a good transition from being inactive to being very active, as in running. Moving fluidly and holding certain postures brings your awareness into your body, allowing for less discursiveness in the mind and more synchronicity—unity of mind and body. Depending on the kind of yoga you do and how you do it, moving fluidly and holding certain postures can bring a new level of awareness. By achieving a level of comfort with your body, you can develop more control and more intimacy with the breath. Controlling the breath allows you to access the mind. Having accessed the mind, you can access wisdom. Even very brief sessions of yoga are beneficial.

In a class, you may be intimidated by other practitioners who are incredibly flexible. However, that is their body, and this is your body. In the beginning, it is not so much about pushing yourself to be flexible as about bringing your mind into the body, which creates a sense of embodiment. Even if you are not engaged in yoga in a deep way, you can still benefit from it by incorporating the mind into the body. Just moving the body into different positions, paying attention and breathing, automatically connects you with natural healthiness and confidence.

19
Confidence

The word *confidence* means to be self-assured about one's qualities. Both running and meditation give us this feeling. In both activities, confidence naturally ensues because we are experiencing self-assurance. Runners know this, because running is an optimistic sport: fundamentally, we believe in the power of the body. Meditation is also an optimistic tradition: fundamentally, we believe in the potential of the mind. In Tibetan, confidence is known as *ziji*. This word can also be translated as "brilliance" or "to shine." *Ziji* expresses how confidence feels and looks: mentally we shine, and physically we glow. Both running and meditation bring out our radiance.

In meditation, *ziji* comes from certainty in our ability to discover our innate awakenment. At a fundamental level, everyone has compassion and egolessness. Thus we say that anyone can attain enlightenment. Although people do stupid things that hurt themselves and others, everyone has that potential. In the Shambhala tradition of warriorship, this limitless potential is known as basic goodness. Through the mind of meditation we develop awareness of this primordial quality. When we have confidence in the warmth and spaciousness of our being, discursive thoughts and emotions are not as problematic, because our view has grown bigger. With this view of basic goodness and the confidence that arises from it, whatever we encounter seems workable.

Without confidence, the hill seems very big, but with confidence, the hill is a little smaller. Without confidence, the avenues of life are blockaded; everything seems like an obstacle. With confidence, our activity becomes a path; we can walk in any direction. Once we know that innate confidence, it is the same whether we are just beginning or are about to enter into the Olympics, and it lasts our whole life.

Confidence arises in the body through physical movement, and in the mind through gaining knowledge. If we do both, that is ideal. There will be times we cannot run because we are injured. Because our body has been our source of confidence, we might feel depressed: physical injury affects our mental confidence as well. However, if we are laid up physically, we can still gain confidence of the mind through knowledge. Gaining mental knowledge is not just keeping the mind occupied with reading, inundating it with useless information. Letting the teachings penetrate our mind requires full engagement.

True confidence is grounded in the unity of mind and body. The two are not meant to be separate. When we only meditate and study, we begin to lose confidence in our physical body. When we only exercise, we begin to lose confidence in our basic goodness and intellect.

Even during our run, we can see the balance of mind and body. It's harder to run when you lose mental confidence. To rearouse it, challenge yourself to accomplish something on the spot: "I'll run to the top of that hill," or "I'll run to that next tree." Or reconsider and refresh your motivation.

Conversely, if your mental confidence is strong and you want to hit the road, but you have not been working out recently, you may lose physical confidence, which begins to weaken your mental confidence. In that case, quell any discouragement by assessing your physical situation. Remind yourself that that after time off, the nerves of the body are a little sluggish and have to be awakened. You may be in even better shape than you feel. Appreciate being alive, and remind yourself that you have the ability to work out once again. No matter what your condition—if you feel you are very out of shape, or even if you feel in shape—the point is to stay in touch with your confidence. You may have made a bad choice, and you may be paying the price, but with mindfulness you can reconnect with your feeling of self-assurance. That's how confidence becomes our secret weapon.

We should wield our confidence wisely, for every situation is an opportunity to do something confidently. At the same time, we should not mix our confidence with a sense of bravado or aggression. The confidence of the tiger does not try to dominate others. Rather, it conquers our own doubt, enhancing our awake and positive qualities.

TIGER CONTEMPLATION: MOTIVATION

In contemplative meditation, we bring a certain thought to mind and focus on it. Just as we use the breath in sitting meditation, this thought becomes the object of our meditation. Contemplating it can help us clarify a question or engender a certain attitude. It can also lead to insight or epiphany or transform our perspective. But the overall reason we practice contemplation is to point our mind in a particular direction.

I recommend that you begin contemplation in the context of formal meditation practice. After sitting for a while in the practice of peaceful abiding, when your mind has settled and is no longer so busy and discursive, bring a contemplative theme to mind. If you've started contemplating too soon, you will know fairly quickly because contemplating exacerbates the thinking process. Many more thoughts arise, which means our mind might become more discursive and therefore less focused. Begin each meditation session by simply following the breath, move on to the contemplation if you can, and then go back to following the breath again, ending the meditation. I have recommended a contemplation for each phase of running—try them if you wish.

In the tiger phase, after assuming a good meditation posture and practicing mindfulness and awareness with presence and attention to the breath, bring to mind the contemplation "What is my motivation?"

If you are a beginner, it's best to keep your motivation simple: to get in shape, to be able to run five or ten miles, or to lose some weight. Or your motivation may be more broad based, like changing your life to become healthier. This could include having a stronger, more flexible mind; being able to sit still for twenty minutes; being less angry; being less affected by negative thoughts; experiencing some mental silence; or beginning to work with the mind and body in earnest. This motivation may grow over the period you are in the tiger phase.

Having determined what your motivation is, stay with that motivation. When your mind gets distracted, come back to that motivation. When the reasons for that motivation begin to dissipate, again think about the reasons that it is helpful and positive. Contemplation is essentially a process of convincing ourselves. We have read books and heard lectures, but now we must make our motivation personal.

After becoming familiar with the process of contemplation during formal meditation, try a version of it while running. It may not necessarily feel the same, but it might help bring a sense of purpose to your run.

You may not be able to focus or go into the contemplation as deeply as when you are sitting quietly, but you will be able to focus a certain amount. In taking your contemplation out for a run, rule number one is to stay mindful. Don't trip or get hit by a car. You should initiate the run by paying attention to the terrain, paying attention to how you feel. Then begin contemplating. During a run of forty-five minutes, five or ten minutes of contemplation is quite a lot. When you come to a certain conclusion or feeling during the contemplation, just keep that motivation in mind, such as running for health. This helps to focus your intention, as well as to train your mind.

As you become more proficient at running, you can expand your motivation to a larger context, such as deciding to run a 10K or a marathon or pinpointing a special route you'd like to complete. If you are an advanced athlete, you might aim at qualifying for in your division, for finals, state or national championships, or even for the Olympics.

As you continue to run, your motivation might enter a deeper phase, in which you are running for a bigger purpose: to understand more about body and mind, exploring themes like "Who am I?" or "What would I like to accomplish in my life?" or "What is the purpose?" These are questions for the dragon, which I'll discuss in Part V.

After the contemplation, simply return to mindfulness and awareness, paying attention to form and enjoying where you are.

PART III

||||||||||||||||||||||||||||||

LION

20
The Sweetness of Virtue

One day, quite naturally and nonchalantly, I found myself slipping on my running shoes and running out the door with ease and pleasure. I realized at that moment, "I must be in shape!" I had entered the lion phase of my training. At the lion stage, we are proficient runners. We are not struggling as much anymore, so the runs are enjoyable. Thanks to the exertion of the tiger, our mind feels invigorated and curious.

Even though my running had been enjoyable most of the way along, I was entering a different territory. Now I could run eighteen to twenty miles whenever I wanted. These distances felt like what running ten miles had felt like before. Running for several hours was delightful. I remember doing several long runs through the mountains of northern Colorado, enjoying the scenery.

The snow lion is a Tibetan creature with a white body and a turquoise mane. This symbol of Tibet embodies delight, discipline, and auspiciousness. Traditionally, the snow lion is pictured holding small cylindrical balls in its paws. These represent the joy and power of the mind. They also represent the virtue that is acquired from hard work.

This lion phase is enjoying the hard work we put into running, capitalizing on all the effort we've put in. It is like planting a flag on a mountaintop. If we don't acknowledge having reached this place, we might become perpetually driven, with no satisfaction. So it's time to take notice that we have accomplished something. Before, our running took more focus and effort; now it comes naturally and easily. We feel almost surprised at how proficient we have become: we enjoy our runs.

In meditation, this phase occurs at the point when our practice is no longer so mechanical. The posture is comfortable; the principles of why we meditate are much clearer. We have worked out the logic and the reasoning. Staying present and following the breath feels more natural than getting lost in our discursiveness; as a result, our discipline keeps getting stronger.

In the beginning, you may have a hard time sitting still for ten minutes and following the breath. Your mind comes and goes many times even in a minute. Now, for thirty, forty, and fifty minutes, your mind stays with the breathing. You may have thoughts, but they are not particularly distracting. This phase of meditation is both peaceful and blissful. Remember, you are not in an alternate universe; you are experiencing the inherent strength and clarity of the mind. It is stable. You are no longer worrying and scampering about. This is how to develop confidence in your inherent good qualities.

In running, the lion phase is when we head out the door without our watch. We are no longer trying to calculate exactly how many miles we run. We are not constantly paying attention to correcting our posture. Rather, we are enjoying being alive, being healthy, being in shape, and being disciplined. We have established our base. Our bones, muscles, and lungs have grown accustomed to running.

Of course, we all run in order to be happy and healthy, but at the lion phase, the joy of running is more consistent. Happiness is a direct result of not struggling with ourselves so much.

As we see in meditation, when we are no longer struggling with ourselves, we are more content, more at peace, and thus happy. We may not necessarily be more enlightened. We may not even be worry-free. But the overall feeling is that we are in a more delightful state of being.

21
Panoramic Awareness

I n the lion phase, we are less focused on the form and technique of our running. Now that we have attained a level of tiger contentment, we need less of our mind to stay focused. Because we have confidence, we are more relaxed, and we need less of our mind to convince ourselves why we are running. What we are doing is now more natural. Running is not simply slogging through the miles, trying to sweat out last night's good times, or burning off excess weight—it is celebrating life.

Even though we must always apply mindfulness, during this phase, instead of just counting breaths or focusing purely on the trail, we train in developing a level of panoramic awareness. With panoramic awareness, we make our mental capability stronger and bigger. With a bigger mind, we are able to understand more. We are able to see things from different perspectives. We are able to be more flexible mentally. We can pick up on how other people think and feel. We might find that we are less irritated when we come home from a run. It takes both skill and relaxation to open ourselves to the environment this way.

The tiger runs have been one pointed. Now our focus is much more expansive: we include our surroundings in our view. Of course, we continue to pay attention to the road, but when we practice panoramic awareness, our consciousness can take in more of the environment. Panoramic awareness is not zoning out, completely distracted by the fantasies in our head. Rather, it is a way to connect to our surroundings, an indication of being alive. It is the healthiness of the mind expressing itself through the healthiness of the body.

Panoramic awareness is not necessarily a dramatic experience. In fact, it might feel quite ordinary. If you are running in the woods, you hear the trees swaying, you see the greenery, you smell the air, and you feel the moisture. If you are in the desert, you taste the dry air, you feel the heat of the sun. If you are in the city, you hear the sound of traffic, you swim in the stream of humanity. Obviously you are not turning your head, constantly looking around—you are still following the route, still moving your arms and legs, still running.

With panoramic awareness, you feel your internal environment—your rhythm, the pounding of your heart, your feet hitting the trail. At the same time, you tune in to your external environment—the sky, the air, the sounds of life. Panoramic awareness is different from being focused on your form. Nor are you simply in your head, struggling with your emotions.

These lion runs are more advanced in that we are sensing ourselves in relationship to where we are. Awareness puts us in tune with the elements. This elemental connection is part of being alive. We are too often indoors, unaware of the elements. The elements are not our enemies: we ourselves are made of the elements. When we connect with them, they inspire us and make us stronger, allowing us to communicate with the world in much subtler ways. This connection occurs when we let ourselves mentally relax into reality: we are not just lonely runners pounding out the miles, but living creatures running on the earth. When we acknowledge that, we feel alive. We do not have to fight our environment.

The lion connects with the elements. First, connecting with the element of wind is important. Our life depends on breathing, taking oxygen into our body. We inhale the environment, and then we exhale, mixing ourselves with the environment. The wind and air are a part of our physical vitality.

As we run, we are also generating heat and fire, earth and water. Our internal body temperature is rising. Heat produced through movement creates energy and sweat. We are sweating water, drinking water, and running on the earth. When we push ourselves off from the earth, we are connecting with the very ground we are running on. We are connecting with our own planet.

We should pay heed to this awareness and become familiar with it. It may sound heady, but panoramic awareness is grounded in what is happening. It is not simply getting high on running, nor does it mean we are devoid of pain. We may have aches and pains, but we can still have panoramic awareness, because now our mind is not completely seduced by that pain.

What we are experiencing is the balance between ourselves and our environment, externally and internally. Previously we were struggling so much internally that we were unaware of our external environment. If somebody asked us to recall the color of a house or what kind of tree we had passed, we might not even remember. But now all those details are vividly clear. It isn't that we didn't want to notice them earlier; rather, we were not in good enough shape to relax. We are no longer physically struggling, and now, through the mind of meditation, we are also more observant. We are much more aware of everything.

This is how the lion dances in the high meadows, frolicking among the peaks and valleys—with panoramic awareness.

22
Healthiness

One of the lessons of the lion is basic healthiness. In meditation, you take the approach from the beginning that the mind is fundamentally healthy and balanced; innately, it has strength and flexibility; it has the ability to love and to be kind. Because of my training, if I feel distracted or tired while I'm meditating, I know that it is not a permanent state; it is just a temporary anomaly, like clouds blocking the sun. The natural state of the mind, basic goodness, is primordial and unchanging.

Approaching meditation with this confidence in the mind's basic goodness, I am able to regain my strength and focus. However, if I feel distracted or tired and decide my mind is hopeless—that I'll never be calm, balanced, or sane—then the more I meditate, the more upset or depressed I might get. So even when I don't feel great, staying in touch with my basic healthiness is a discipline I try to observe in both running and meditation.

In running, regarding yourself as basically healthy is how to avoid getting trapped in a negative state of mind, thinking you are weak or out of shape. It may be true that you cannot run five or ten miles right now, but you should recognize the fact that your healthiness is innate. Being in shape is within us, as if we were small birds ready to fly. Genetically, the bird is predisposed to flying. Likewise, we are designed to move.

My father was an inspiration in this regard. He was a great meditation master. While escaping from Tibet, he walked out of the Himalayas. Somehow that kept him fit for life. He never exercised very much, but he always approached things from the point of view of basic healthiness. Therefore, he always had a vigor and energy about him.

The lineage that I received and now hold began with the Buddha over twenty-five-hundred years ago. When we hear the Buddha's name, a saintly individual comes to mind. He was anointed as *buddha*, "the awakened one," in the sixth century BC. Having attained a state of mind in which he experienced ultimate reality, he then proceeded to teach about his experience for the next fifty years, finally passing away at the age of eighty-four.

Despite this incredible spiritual accomplishment, before his spiritual life even began, the Buddha was quite an athlete, accomplished in javelin throwing, wrestling, archery, and charioteering. He was tall, extremely handsome, and well proportioned, with "the chest of a lion and calves like an antelope," according to tradition. In other words, he was a very athletic fellow. Thus the Buddha was quite well suited to talk about both physical and mental disciplines, as ideally one would have both these elements in one's life. Meditation, much like running, was considered to be a good and healthy exercise—for the mind.

What meditators have known for centuries is that the mind is raw material. It's like tofu—neutral and pliable. The mind has two basic modes of receiving experiences that alter how it feels. One is the outside environment, which comes through our five senses: what we see, touch, hear, taste, and smell. All those feelings and experiences get absorbed into the mind. The other feelings are what the mind thinks, either internally, or in relation to what is coming from the outside. This is our sixth consciousness, which is the mental consciousness.

Like the body, without direction, the mind begins to absorb any habits that are in its environment. For example, if somebody yells something aggressive at you, that aggression gets absorbed. If those aggressive remarks are experienced as painful, you will most likely respond with aggression. If your mind is more flexible, you might feel sorry for the other person and say something kind, or nothing at all. Conversely, when someone says "I love you," that too is absorbed. If you feel pleasure, you might respond by saying, "I love you, too." On the other hand, if you feel paranoid, threatened, or scared because you do not feel ready to tie the knot, you might try to change the subject. These elements are coming from the outside.

The mind also absorbs habits from our internal environment. For example, you may be happily sitting on a park bench, fairly oblivious to children laughing, kites in the air, people playing football. You are by yourself in your mind, thinking away. If you are thinking how things are going well at work, your mind is having thoughts of satisfaction, and you feel good. If you are worrying about paying your rent or keeping your relationship, you might feel anxious and fearful. This is regardless of the children playing, the sun shining, or the birds singing in the trees.

In both cases, the external environment had little to do with how you felt. How you felt was totally dependent on the thoughts being generated in your mind. So you see the power of thoughts, and, in particular and most important, you see the power of the appearance of some thoughts and the absence of other thoughts.

In other words, if you are thinking about something such as work or family, it makes you feel good or bad depending on what is happening in those scenarios. Thus the practice of meditation is being clearly aware, first of the power of the mind—what the mind experiences and how you feel; and second, of the power of thoughts—what the mind is engaged in. Similarly, the practice of meditation has to do with the power of nonthoughts—what the mind is not engaged in.

What meditators have discovered by observing the mind is that the mind is a living, changing, developing creature. The mind is incredibly sensitive and, at the same time, incredibly tough. Both moved by the simple beauty of a butterfly fluttering past and able to adapt to extremely severe scenarios, somehow the human mind survives. It is also capable of incredible generosity and compassion. Most important, the mind can be trained. It can be worked with and developed. Meditators have discovered that the mind even enjoys being developed and trained, given the right tutor.

As with the body, the effects of how you are treating the mind are felt immediately. If you mistreat your body by not exercising; by overeating, smoking, or drinking; or by subjecting it to weather, general stress, or travel, you begin to feel stiff, achy, tired, and lethargic. With the body, we are not that surprised.

The mind is no different. If we subject the mind to prolonged periods of watching television or sitting at the computer, or even more potentially harmful environments such as feeling unloved or uncared for, or if we are subjected to long periods of dissatisfaction or intensely aggressive environments, the mind takes a beating. That piece of tofu is turning many colors. It is being bruised and battered, but we cannot see this happening.

If the environment is negative, then, generally speaking, we are in an unhappy state of mind. You might not overtly say, "I'm unhappy," but you might say, "I don't feel like myself," or "I feel slightly off." If it is a little more severe, you might feel slightly depressed and unmotivated. If it is a little more extreme, you might feel bitterness and resentment. Of course, if it is more extreme, there is the constant feeling of being agitated and angry.

Conversely, if you put your mind into positive environments, such as love and affection, satisfaction, accomplishment, and purpose, then you immediately feel those effects. Likewise, in a positive environment, your mind will feel buoyant. You will be curious and interested in what is happening around you. You will be quicker to laugh or smile. You will also be quicker to feel the emotions of others—and your kindness, empathy, and love will be more readily available.

Of course, these are very basic generalizations, and within them there are many different combinations of possibilities. But underneath all of it lies the principle of basic healthiness. The meditation tradition acknowledges the fact that life is impermanent, unsure, and unstable: we are certain to find ourselves in a number of scenarios. But we can tap into an internal level of health and stability by relating to our mind. That in a nutshell is essentially what meditation practice is: creating a personal, self-contained environment in which you develop health and happiness for your mind. That's where the lion's discipline enters the picture.

When I visited Tibet, the climate was harsh, and people often had a weathered look, but everyone demonstrated this basic healthiness and strength. When people were sick, they would come to me for a blessing, but I never heard them complaining. Instead, they always talked about what parts of themselves still worked. This struck me as unusual, because in the modern world, we have more medicine, but we also seem to have more complaining. There is a general sense of hypochondria.

Runners, possibly more than anyone else, fall into this trap. When we're running and we feel a twinge, we often think that it is the beginning of the end. This is overmindfulness bordering on paranoia. Once we get into this overly analytical state of mind, we become superheightened, not for the positive, but for the negative. It is hard to eat a good meal or have a conversation, much less get over a strenuous run, because we are fixated on what is wrong—or on what could be wrong. But if we cultivate the discipline to remember our basic healthiness and relax, we will be able to enjoy any activity we engage in. This does not mean that we forget about improvement, for a basic sense of healthiness gives us the ability to see our weak areas and improve upon them. But with the joy and discipline of the lion, we are coming from a place of strength.

23
How to Deal with Pain

When people say they don't like running, often what they are saying is that they don't like pain. Running is a sport that is continuously laden with pain; that's why it gives us character. Sometimes I can tell if someone is going to stay with running: they like the pain, but not too much.

After I developed an enormous blister on my foot while running my first marathon, a few runners asked me how I had dealt with the pain. Some of them implied that I must have been doing some secret meditation to block it out. I explained to them that I was not blocking it out: I was paying attention to the pain, but at the same time, I did not allow it to steal my mind. The pain was an important part of the reality, but worrying excessively was not going to accomplish anything.

One could say that life is at least 50 percent pain. If we do not relate to pain, we are not relating to half our life. Everything is fine when we are happy, but when we are in pain, we become petrified. The inability to relate to pain narrows our playing field. When we are able to work with pain and understand it, life becomes twice as interesting. Relating to pain makes us more fearless and happy.

Physically, everyone experiences bodily pain. In fact, the practice of yoga was partially designed to make the body flexible so that one could remain motionless in order to meditate.

The more supple our body, the more comfortable it is, and the less pain we feel. But even with great flexibility, the body cannot remain in one position for long, so day and night we are shifting positions. By the same token, everyone worries, and there is not a single person who does not have a level of regret. This creates mental pain. Mental pain and worry are responsible for many of our other pains.

Meditation and running are essentially addressing these two kinds of pain. Of course, we cannot run all day and all night, and it is difficult to meditate all day and all night. However, when we include these two disciplines in our daily routine, we are making our body and mind more livable.

The lion deals with pain cheerfully. That does not mean suppressing it: there is an appropriate balance. We will be working with this balance for the rest of our lives. If we are constantly complaining about how we feel and what kind of pain we are in, people will want to avoid us. If we are ill, of course we should let others know. But otherwise, it's better to keep your pain to yourself.

In dealing with pain, there are a few different factors to understand. First, pain—and therefore sickness—is usually the result of different circumstances coming together. When I developed a blister on my foot at the Toronto Marathon, it was the result of a decision I had made to wear new socks that day. As well, there was a slight drizzle, so between the friction and the dampness, I was experiencing pain.

On the walls of Tibetan monasteries, one often sees a mural called the wheel of life, in which each phase of life is depicted by an image. Associated with sickness and attachment is the image of someone shot with an arrow. The wisdom that accompanies this image is that when you are shot by an arrow, you do not ask who made the arrow, what kind of wood the arrow was made from, or what technique was used to make its tip. The question is, How you are going to take the arrow out?

Ignoring the pain takes enormous mental effort. The first step is to acknowledge the pain. The pain is one thing, and the mind reacting to the pain is another, so the second step is not to overreact. Becoming startled by the pain only exacerbates the pain, like throwing gasoline on a fire: our reaction to the pain makes it even worse. Therefore we acknowledge the pain, but we avoid having the immediate reactionary response.

As I have said earlier, consciousness is neutral. It absorbs whatever it experiences—happiness or unhappiness, pain or health. The well-being of our consciousness is our own responsibility. It is very simple: if we are perpetually grumpy, then after a while, grumpiness becomes our state of mind. Then even good things make us grumpy. This is simply the only result that can occur.

Pain and sickness are clear indications that something is off-balance. They are signals from reality. We made bad choices, we ate wrong, or we were not mindful, and now we are feeling the effects. Taking responsibility is not blaming the pain or anything else. Simultaneously, you don't need to feel guilty or chastise yourself. Blame combined with pain only infects the pain with negativity.

If we are overwhelmed by pain and unhappiness, we often react in a childish way: we objectify the pain. As soon as we start accusing the pain, the pain becomes our enemy. Getting angry does not help us grow from the experience.

Rather, we can recognize our actions and rectify them. This allows us to use pain as a way to support our own growth and integrity. Acknowledging that something is off is a sign of maturity. Recognizing that pain is an opportunity to grow gives us the power to see how to correct the imbalance and move forward, taking on the pain as a journey. Then we see pain as an opportunity. If we trip and fall, we see that as an opportunity to be more mindful in the future. If we spend the whole time thinking about it and magnifying the pain, then negativity just grows in us. If we see how it happened, we can learn from it without dwelling on it.

When I was developing that blister, I acknowledged the pain. To disempower it, I saw it as a clear sign that something was out of balance. All I could do at that point was to focus on my inherent strength and the fitness I had achieved. My approach was not stupid, for I knew this was not a major injury—I would survive. In that way, I associated my mind with thoughts that would strengthen my resolve to finish the race. Focusing my mind just on the pain would have slowly drained all my energy, eventually leading me to think that I could not continue.

Likewise, in meditation we experience physical pain as well as pain from thoughts and emotions, but we cannot let this suffering completely rule our mind. If we do, the pain sabotages any benefit we might gain from our practice, and the whole session becomes a meditation on our suffering. If we are in physical pain, we can shift our position. If we are in emotional pain, we can disassemble that emotion methodically until it releases its hold. If we are being tortured by thoughts, we can make our perspective bigger by remembering our skylike mind or by lifting our gaze and looking around the room. We relate to this emotional pain in a very straightforward way.

It is helpful to regard the experience of pain as a way to stay connected with others. Everybody suffers. When our own pain serves as a reminder of this truth, we can use it as a source of genuine compassion. The lion knows that underneath the pain lies fundamental healthiness and basic goodness. Even when it hurts, you can promote that attitude by turning your mind to its natural radiance and generating compassion for others.

24

Running and Meditating to Refresh

Running is a basic, natural movement—simply placing one foot in front of the other—but when we look at its biomechanics, it becomes more complicated. Similarly, meditation is quite simple and straightforward—the act of being present, one moment after another. Yet, in Tibet, thousands of texts have been written on this subject.

However, if we apply the simplicity of meditation to our mind, even after a long day, it can certainly benefit our well-being. Meditating after a long day allows the mind to cleanse itself and regain some strength, resilience, and joy. We take our attention from the day and place our mind in the stillness of the moment. By not overthinking or daydreaming, we relieve the mind of fantasies and worries, and we can just be present.

The mind behaves in a dualistic fashion. An image comes to mind—a project at work or marital issues—and we respond to that image. Perhaps our response is to feel guilt. If we have fantasies, we may feel desire. Or we see a rock, and, mistaking it for a dog, we feel fear. The mind is constantly reacting to and associating with these thoughts and images. That's why we feel tired, overworked, or irritated. Paying attention to our breathing and being present, our mind has the space to relax.

Imagine that your mind is like your hand, holding a

dumbbell. That dumbbell is all your issues and concerns. Being present in meditation is like putting the dumbbell down. Immediately there is less stress in the body and mind. Meditation works in gradations. First, we try to let go of the bigger thoughts and concerns, alleviating the mind of that weight. It's like taking the backpack off during an uphill hike—it allows us to recover our energy. Then we let go of the smaller thoughts and concerns.

Conversely, after a day at work, if we take on more thoughts and concerns, that is not resting. If we come home from our day and immediately turn on the television to watch the news, we become overburdened by hearing about the various tragedies that are going on all over the world. Even though those global concerns are very important, what is more important at that moment is relieving the mind of overload and stress.

Often what people like about watching television and movies is that it allows them to temporarily exchange their personal concerns for those of others. The news of something happening far away has a less immediate effect than what is happening in our own life: we are distracted from our own mental concerns. We feel a certain amount of relief, but it does not allow the mind to fully rest, relax, and rejuvenate. According to the meditation tradition, the negative visual images we see and the emotions associated with them go deep into our consciousness.

In the meditative tradition, there are said to be eight levels of consciousness. The first five are associated with the five sense perceptions. The sixth consciousness is the mental consciousness, the thinking consciousness, which has dreams and memories. The seventh consciousness is the emotional consciousness. Then, there is the eighth consciousness, which is the base consciousness that includes all the others. It is said that the eighth consciousness is where images and actions are stored. In the West, this is sometimes referred to as the subconscious.

The longer we live, the more images we collect, both positive and negative. These images are not always at the front of our mind; they fall to the background of our mind. But when we have a buildup of images, especially of negative ones, they come to mind more and more as bothersome thoughts, wreaking havoc on our sleep and our relationships. Since the mind is neutral and adapts to its environment, we become accustomed to this experience, like becoming accustomed to dirt and clutter in an unkempt house. A rundown and irritated feeling becomes the norm, and after a while, we can't imagine feeling a different way. We just assume that nobody is happy because we are not.

We can use meditation as a cleansing process—the time of the day that we do our mental laundry. Doing the laundry, we feel fresh and uplifted. Therefore, after a long day, take ten, twenty, or thirty minutes to meditate. Sitting there, placing the mind on the breath instead of on your worries, you are developing the ability to alleviate your stress and strengthen your mind. Then try applying that skill to your running by placing your mind on the environment rather than on your thinking process.

This is how to give your mind and body a relaxing and rejuvenating break. Let them discover their innate intelligence and well-being. The next time you come home from work, instead of turning on the television or going online, sit and meditate for ten or twenty minutes. As you switch allegiance from the concerns of the day to the health of your mind, know that by being present even for ten seconds, thirty seconds, a minute, or two minutes, you are enabling a great weight to be lifted from your mind. Your mind is being cleansed because you are bathing in the moment. In this way, you are coming into contact with your big, naturally healthy mind. As you rest in that strength, you are becoming more open-minded and caring.

Then go for a run. Let your sense perceptions, your connection to the elements, and the movement of your body enter you into the larger world. Know that with the discipline of being present in your run, you are purifying your mind, allowing its natural qualities to shine.

25
Happiness

After the publication of my book *Ruling Your World* in 2005, I teamed up with Queen Noor of Jordan and Rabbi Irwin Kula to conduct a panel on compassionate leadership. We three leaders of different backgrounds came together to discuss how compassion is essential to strong leadership. We presented our panel at New York University and Tufts University, since we felt that the future would benefit from young people hearing this discussion. Jerry Murdock, a fellow runner and meditator, acted as moderator, and Goldman Sachs hosted us as well. Although it was a very busy and exciting time, I was able to fit in my runs and my meditation.

Like many people, after a busy time, I enjoy a good run. After long days of meetings or teaching without much movement, I make the effort to run. By engaging in this healthy activity, I feel happier afterward. Likewise, after applying myself mentally to positive thoughts, I meditate on compassion. By extending my mind toward others, naturally I feel more delighted. Engaging in movement and meditation is the ticket to physical and mental happiness. We may not want to do it, but it is good for us.

In the lion phase, you should get familiar with and accustomed to happiness. Do not be afraid it is going to disappear. Have trust in its naturalness. This happiness is the natural screen saver of the mind. There is no point in dragging in worrisome e-mails or surfing the Net for entertainment and distraction. Just relax and feel good. This may sound indulgent, but it is how we develop strength and confidence in our basic state of being. It is important to recognize how happiness feels and to realize that it is natural and healthy.

It is okay to be happy. We do not need to feel guilty about our enjoyment. At the same time, when we know how basic goodness feels, we realize that happiness is not some elated state of being. It does not mean we are constantly telling jokes. It does not require cajoling, because it is already there in our innate intelligence, curiosity, and appreciation. With the snow lion's delight, we are simply feeling the natural health of the mind. We will know when we get too attached to this happiness, because it will transform into desire and obsession.

The secret to long-term happiness is engaging in activities that are healthy, mentally and physically. Physical happiness comes from good movement, good posture, drinking water, and eating good, healthy food. Physical unhappiness comes from stagnation, nonmovement, bad posture, poor-quality food, not enough liquid, and a lack of oxygen. Mental happiness comes from mentally healthy engagements such as love, generosity, and compassion. Mental unhappiness comes from self-centeredness, anger, pride, extreme mental states, excessive emotions, and too much discursiveness.

In the lion phase, the happiness that we experience is not coming out of nowhere. It is the result of physical discipline and mental exertion. Therefore happiness is not a goal, but a by-product of mentally and physically healthy activities. If we engage in these, happiness of mind and body will ensue.

Letting yourself become genuinely connected with happiness allows you to also deal with sadness. If your mind is obsessed with happiness, you might react to sadness by getting depressed or angry. I've learned that the best way to be happy is not to have happiness as your objective. If you crave personal happiness, it only becomes more elusive. In fact, making happiness your personal goal is a direct ticket to unhappiness, because you become centered on "me." One of my favorite sayings is "If you want to be miserable, think of yourself. If you want to be happy, think of others." When you are self-obsessed, what makes "me" happy is short lived.

Often what is healthy for us may not initially feel good. That's because we have habituated ourselves to do unhealthy things. The mind and body can easily habituate to negative habits as well as to positive habits. The result of negative habits is unhappiness, and the result of positive habits is happiness. After a long day of being indoors at the office, getting changed and going for a run sometimes feels like it takes too much effort. Just watching television seems more compatible. But if our goal in watching television is to be happy, we should remember that happiness comes from healthy activities. So we should change and go for a run, or turn off the television and go meditate.

Thirty minutes of moving our body or thirty minutes of meditating on compassion lead to vitality and happiness. The more we understand this, the more we do it. The more we do it, the healthier it feels. Through healthy activity, happiness of body and mind becomes the continuum. We begin to understand that unhappiness is simply the result of wrong engagement. We are engaged in activities that are not leading anywhere, or we have given up to some degree. Thus we must keep our discipline. We are discovering that far from making us into drudges, discipline brings joy—because it teaches which activities to cultivate and which to discard.

The sixth-century Buddhist Indian meditation master Shantideva said that when we exert ourselves toward positive endeavors, we should not grimace, but rather have the joy of an elephant jumping into a pool of cool water on a hot, dusty day. This analogy inspires me because when we are working toward good things, it is not always easy. In fact, it can be downright painful. I think about that elephant when I am about to sit down for ten days or a month of meditation. These days can be eighteen hours long. We have to rise at two thirty in the morning to start by three, and our meditations and liturgical chanting may not be over until ten at night. But rarely do I wake up depressed about it. Usually I feel enthusiastic.

Chanting and meditating hour after hour, whether the room is freezing cold or unbearably hot, I have an attitude of enthusiasm because my activity is for a good purpose. Not only am I deepening my understanding, my discipline also helps others. Some of the rituals involve praying for sick people. Annually, the monasteries do long practices for peace and the general health and welfare of all beings.

I have applied this kind of exertion to my running and exercise on countless cold early mornings and sweltering hot afternoons—often my only opportunity to run when I'm teaching, or studying at the monastery. I try to approach the cold or heat or my exhaustion with the joy of that elephant, because I know I am doing something good.

Like many runners, rarely do I regret a run. With the lion's joy and discipline, I can run in almost any situation. One winter I was training for the Miami Half Marathon. I was in Cape Breton, one of the easternmost points in North America. It is a stunningly beautiful island, with moose roaming about and bald eagles perching high on the trees. The island has Acadian roots and is famous for Celtic fiddling, but I was not there for a ceilidh. I was doing a meditation retreat. I had found a way to sneak in some runs, and I still had one long run to do before the race.

The night before my long run, a blizzard blew in. The next morning, Josh Silberstein, my assistant, who was training for his first full marathon, was quite disappointed that we were not able to run. But looking outside, I saw that the snow had stopped, revealing a fantastically white wonderland under clear, blue skies. So I said, "Let's go."

We put our running shoes in plastic bags and headed out on snowshoes. It took us forty-five minutes just to wade down the long driveway in waist-high snow. Finally we reached the road, which was completely silent; thankfully a snowplow had already come through. Then we proceeded to go for a two-hour run. As we ran through the village of Ingonish, people were amused to see us running by, and we waved. The snowfall had created a cheerful, cozy atmosphere.

When we landed in Miami a few days later, the temperature was eighty-five degrees. Nobody could have guessed where we had just been training. Both Josh and I successfully completed our races. Josh was happy, and so was I—the result of knowing how to apply our discipline and joy.

26
Pride

n the snow lion phase of meditation, the joy we feel comes from accomplishing a level of egolessness. In practicing mindfulness and awareness, we have let go of some of our baggage. The chip on our shoulder is smaller. We have reduced the weight of our worries. We can think more clearly and run faster. With ego, we are too big to fit anywhere. With egolessness, we can go anywhere. The practice of panoramic awareness has connected us to a larger world, and we see that we are part of it.

Being mentally and physically lighter allows us to ascend to the high meadows of the Himalayas and smell the sweet, fragrant air. We are proud to be in such good shape. We may even become arrogant about it. This is a potential downfall in the lion phase.

The Buddhist tradition identifies five kinds of pride. First is the pride that comes from position: you come from an important family, you have been promoted to an important position, or you consider yourself part of an elite group. The next pride comes from wealth, which could relate to money or to acquiring new possessions like a car or clothing. Third is intellectual pride: you are proud because of what you know. The next pride comes from prowess, youth, or beauty. An athlete is particularly prone to this kind of pride because it results from physical appearance. When your mind and body are in prime condition, there is always some pride. The last category is pride resulting from thinking that you do not have pride.

Pride is mental bloatedness based on an inaccurate self-assessment: we have overvalued ourselves. If we were an economy, it would be inflated. It is said that with the acquisition of pride, all other previous virtues such as gentleness and discipline are nullified. Being full of ourselves leaves no room for the good qualities we worked so hard to develop. Pride is obviously annoying to the people around us because it makes us blind to their virtues. It can also be quite dangerous for us in ways that pave the road to ruin.

If we won the Nobel Prize in a scientific discipline, it is unlikely that we would trip and fall, forgetting all our math. But as runners, the basis of our pride is much more fragile, since it rests on having a healthy body. If we pull a muscle, we could be out for months. We should avoid being proud snow lions, obsessed with ourselves.

Pride may not show up all at once. We feel like we are in good shape, so we don't need to train as much. We think that the less challenging runs are beneath us. Our pride tricks us into taking our fitness for granted. As soon as that occurs, being in shape starts slipping away. Thus the obvious antidote to pride is humbleness. The lion uses humbleness to stay grounded, less prone to tripping or falling.

Humbleness always looks good coupled with success. But success anointed with pride appears ostentatious. When we accomplish our goals, obviously we are going to feel proud—as we should. But the pride we are discussing here is more a disease than a celebration.

Humor is a good way to keep our pride in check. Humor indicates being open. We're not always cracking jokes or pulling pranks, but we have a flexible attitude. Running and meditation constantly lead us to a state of openness, so if we find ourselves feeling attached to our accomplishments, we may want to interject some humor. We could spend some time with friends and lighten up. This helps our mind and our attitude and it inevitably helps our meditation. Being able to laugh—particularly at ourselves—is a survival tool for life.

In Tibetan, pride is *ngagyal,* which translates as "I am great." This is different from "I feel great," which has more to do with confidence. Confidence is the outgrowth of positive qualities, whereas pride is the outgrowth of negative qualities among positive qualities. Therefore, in the lion phase, it is important to enjoy what we have accomplished, but we should check our egos at the door.

LION CONTEMPLATION: GOOD FORTUNE

During the lion phase, we contemplate feeling fortunate. Even though we may have difficult days, if we are running and meditating, we probably have a lot to be grateful for. Appreciating who we are and what we have energizes our vitality, strength, and purpose. Thinking about what we do not have leads us down the road of negativity and despair. We can feel grateful for our good health and ability to exercise, our relatively sane mind, and our sense faculties. By contemplating these truths, we come to the conclusion that we are fortunate.

First of all, we are alive. Many of us here in the West live in countries that are relatively stable, politically and economically. We have the freedom to think and do what we want. We live in houses that are heated and cooled. We have the company of friends and family. For the most part, we have access to good medical care.

As you contemplate your good fortune, you might find yourself having thoughts like "I live in America, but I'd rather live in Canada," "I make good money, but I'm not as wealthy as so-and-so," or "I'm healthy, but I wish I were ten years younger." When this occurs, be aware that you've stopped contemplating your good fortune and started contemplating regret. Try to stay in the present. You are training and developing your mind. Contemplating your good fortune, you feel delighted and special. This feeling makes you want to use your life wisely. As a result, after doing this contemplation, you tend to be more appreciative of what you do have, and to spend less time wishing things were another way. Therefore you waste less time.

When we feel fortunate, we inevitably want to move in a

positive direction. With this attitude, it is easier to change bad habits. We find it easier to apologize to someone than to hold a grudge, which wastes energy. The work that we do, we do well, instead of wishing there were another way.

In feeling fortunate, a deep and profound appreciation develops in us. Thus, as we become more familiar with appreciation, it begins to become our character. This contemplation is quite important, especially these days, when there is so much advertising telling us what we don't have and showing us what we are missing. The message of most advertising is that the product will make us feel special and happy, and therefore we will feel content and fortunate. The reality is that we do not need to buy another thing or go to another place in order to have those feelings. We can discover the fortunateness of the here and now.

To those of us in this busy world of many choices, contemplating our good fortune may seem simple minded or even naïve. Yet this meditation is so powerful that I have heard meditators with only one set of clothing and enough food for a day talk about how fortunate they are. And when I work with people who are sick and dying, this attitude of fortunateness is very powerful for them in two ways. First, almost always they feel regret at having wasted so much time not appreciating what they had, always striving. In their final days, they also often realize that none of us knows how much time we really have, and therefore we should appreciate the present moment. With their remaining days, they feel fortunate for what they have now.

Generating a feeling of fortunateness doesn't have to become too heavy a meditation, or an overly belabored process. We can simply use it to remind us that we're lucky to be alive.

In bringing this contemplation on a run, we can do it with

an added emphasis on how fortunate we are to be able to run, to be healthy, to be outdoors, or to find a working treadmill.

Whether your sense of good fortune is small or large does not matter, for every moment of appreciation you feel adds up. Especially after a run, most of us feel appreciative—and we can bring that appreciation into our entire life.

PART IV

GARUDA

27
Garuda

Having established ourselves at the tiger level through mindfulness and gentleness in building our base, we have savored the delight and discipline of the lion phase. Now we enter the outrageous part of our training, the garuda phase. Throughout Asian culture, the garuda is depicted as a mythical bird with human arms that hatches ready to fly. This phase of running is "outrageous" because we are ready to challenge ourselves to go beyond our comfort zone.

The technique for the garuda run is experiencing a new environment, which enables you to experience new and fresh stimuli. You might therefore run in a new location. Since this run is challenging, it will take all of your physical and mental power. It is good to remind yourself of the basics: aligning your posture, working with the breath, and placing your feet properly. This mindfulness will give you the strength to complete your challenging run. At the same time, incorporate the panoramic experience from the lion phase. Thus you have both an attention to detail and an appreciation of the environment.

The meditation technique of the garuda is moving forward with a healthy balance of mindfulness and awareness, with the result that we can surpass previous limitations. When we are at the outrageous stage of our meditation, we may want to challenge ourselves by doing a longer session. If we are used to doing twenty minutes to a half an hour, we may want to try an hour or more. We often have longer sessions as well, which are known in Tibetan as *nyinthün* or *dathün*. *Thün* means a period of time. Thus *nyinthün* means a full day of meditation. *Dawa* is the word for moon, and thus *dathün* means one month of meditation.

At many of the Shambhala centers, we conduct these day-long, week-long, or month-long meditations. These sessions begin in the morning and are broken up by frequent and some-times not-so-frequent walking breaks and meal breaks. These intensive meditation sessions are challenging, but therein lies the benefit.

I equate these longer meditation sessions to great expeditions. If we decide to explore a new country and we go for just an hour, we only get a taste of our destination. If we go for one day, we experience so much more: we have time to learn a little about the culture and the people. However, if we go for one month, the place we are visiting becomes familiar. These meditation sessions are therefore opportunities to experience and discover our mind, becoming familiar with ourselves. By participating in a *nyinthün* or *dathün*, we are vacationing at home. These longer sessions are excellent for gaining proficiency in the practice of meditation, for reaching a deeper knowledge and understanding of its purpose. We can begin to see how we can shift habitual mental patterns, which can result in bigger changes.

In running, this garuda phase is helpful because it can break you out of a rut. It can help you surpass what you thought you were able to do. It is always good to have a challenge, even a minor one. Thus in this outrageous phase, pick a goal that challenges you. It is important to understand what "outrageous" means. It is not doing something dangerous or potentially harmful—that would denote an outrageous level of stupidity. The garuda is outrageous with a level of intelligence. It could be as simple as running beyond your norm in terms of time or distance.

After I had run several marathons, instead of running another marathon and trying to beat my own time, I chose to challenge myself in a different way. Wanting to do something that was difficult but not impossible, I decided to do a thirty-two-mile ultramarathon. Since there was no convenient race I could fit into my schedule, I created a mini ultramarathon, to take place in northern Colorado. I discussed this with some of my running colleagues, and everyone was eager to participate.

The Tibetan word for outrageous is *p'hotso,* which means "determined estimation." In other words, we know what our outer limits are. I knew my outer limit was probably thirty miles or so. Trying to run a hundred-mile ultra at that point would not have been outrageous for me—it would have been unrealistic and potentially dangerous. "Outrageous" includes good judgment and, at the same time, challenge.

The morning of the ultramarathon we woke up early, so as not to be finishing the ultra in the midday sun. I ate my favorite prerun breakfast of blueberry oat muffins, and then we drove to the drop-off point.

I had invited Mike Sandrock, the Boulder *Daily Camera*'s running writer, to join us. He thought it might make an interesting story. The rest of us were all excited about the big run ahead, but Mike is always like a character out of a samurai movie—the well-worn warrior who takes everything in stride. I was amused that morning because he was the last one to get out of bed.

Our route consisted of a twenty-three-mile loop with a ten-mile finish that would lead us back to Shambhala Mountain

Center, a retreat center located near Red Feather Lakes, Colorado, and its Great Stupa of Dharmakaya—a 108-foot monument to peace and enlightenment that attracts visitors from around the world. The terrain we would run was hilly, remote, and very beautiful.

The whole group was filled with the kind of anticipation that is often present at the beginning of a long run. We intuitively knew that this run—a culmination of much training and discipline—was important for everyone. Now we were all here, being present. Beginning the run in pitch black on a dirt road in the dark had an exciting as well as an ominous feeling. Several people wore headlamps. As we ran through the hills in the dark, we could hear one another's breathing. By the time dawn broke, we had already been running for a while, and the sunrise was a welcome sign. At the same time, it was a harbinger of the intense Colorado summer sun to come.

Continuing our run, we headed down into a valley, dropping from an altitude of 8,500 feet to 7,500 feet. At the valley bottom, we ran some through beautiful canyons. Then we hit the dreaded "death valley"—a long, winding hill that lasts for six miles. This was the most challenging part of the run.

Miles nineteen through twenty-one were straight uphill, eventually taking us back up to 9,000 feet. Once we crested the high point, we hit a slow descent all the way back to the meditation center. Ironically, this was the easiest part of the run. We all had great energy, and even at that altitude, we were making good time.

As we made our way up to the Great Stupa, people were lining the roads and cheering us on. We grabbed a *lungta* prayer flag and finally reached the stupa, finishing with the traditional Shambhala warrior's victory cry—*"Ki ki so so!"* It felt strange to finally stop running after more than five hours.

This ultramarathon had clearly tested my limits. Previously I had been able to run twenty-six miles, and pushing it beyond thirty was doable, but here I was stretching the boundaries. This was my outrageous run. My body definitely felt the challenge, and my inner limits were challenged as well.

However, I had prepared myself properly. In the previous weeks, I had run eighteen miles on one day and sixteen miles the next day, adding up to thirty-four miles in a forty-eight-hour period. So I knew my body would be able to handle running over thirty miles in one day. Mentally, I had weighed the pros and cons of doing such a long run, knowing that I might hurt myself. Finally, when I had determined that I was in good enough shape to use my fitness in this way, I also utilized the run to raise money for charity, so there was an element of emotional satisfaction as well.

After this run, I talked to some people who said they could not even conceive of running for that long; they could only run for a few miles. I told them that I was like them a few short years ago. In fact, running six miles had felt like running thirty. I was only able to run the ultra because I had challenged myself all along the way.

28
Beyond Hope and Fear

The garuda, like the phoenix in the Chinese tradition or the eagle in the seal of the United States or the Roman Empire, can represent power and authority. But in the meditation tradition of Tibet, it represents balance and freedom. The spread wings of the garuda indicate the balance between focused mindfulness and panoramic awareness. Since a bird can fly in all directions, it has a large view, which gives it the ability to accurately assess situations. The garuda in particular symbolizes freedom from hope and fear—our hoping that something will happen and being fearful that it will not.

Hope and fear stem from two kinds of pain: the pain of not encountering what we want, and the pain of encountering what we don't want. We often experience the pleasure of getting something we want and the pain of encountering something we don't want. We go to a restaurant, and they are out of the special dish we wanted. All that's left is the tofuburger, which we did not want. Sports in general offer a rudimentary example of hope and fear: we hope to win, and we fear that we will lose. In running, we are constantly besieged by hope and fear. Meditation is also a good example of the experience of hope and fear: we hope to have deep realization, and we fear that we will not.

Especially for the runner and the meditator, how the mind

handles pain and pleasure is extremely important. As I have said, the mind in its most basic form is a neutral entity. We can compare it to going to the movies. If it's a horror movie, the mind is unable to handle the pain and tries to get away from it. We may even want to leave the theater. Conversely, if it's a good romantic comedy, the mind cannot get enough. We don't want the movie to stop. When the mind experiences pleasure, it does not want to be separated from that pleasure. If we watch our mind, we can see these two principles happening.

In relating to pain, it is not so much the pain that is difficult—it is the inability of the mind to handle the pain. In meditation, people are often unable to handle the pain of the posture, disturbing thoughts, or boredom. It is not the boredom itself that is painful but the mind's inability to handle it. Often, what exasperates the mind is the mind itself becoming hysterical: we are unable to handle both the pain and a hysterical mind. So when pain arises in either meditation or running, we need to feel the difference between the pain itself and the mind's inability to handle the pain—or, in the case of a trained mind—our ability to handle it.

Conversely, if the situation is pleasurable, the mind wants more pleasure. In meditation this is known as "the seduction of calm states"—all the meditator wants is to experience peace and tranquillity. The mind becomes attached to the meditative pleasures, and therefore pleasurable mental states. In running, we get addicted to the runner's high. As we receive more pleasure, the mind essentially gets addicted. When we are separated from that pleasure, we may become depressed or even angry, which is painful because we can't handle the fear of losing our object of pleasure. Whether we are running too much or meditating only to experience pleasurable states, we naturally turn something beneficial into something problematic.

Throughout life it is inevitable that we will experience both pain and pleasure. Learning how to handle them leads to harmony and happiness. In meditation, if we are unable to handle pain or boredom, then that pain or boredom becomes our master. Then we spend our entire life trying to avoid being bored or feeling pain. However if we can handle our mind, then we know that we can handle boredom and pain.

Conversely if we are seduced by pleasure, then pleasure rules our lives. However, if we appreciate and enjoy our mind, then we do not find ourselves constantly in the pursuit of pleasure. This gives us a healthy sense of independence, which benefits both our meditation and our running.

This freedom liberates us from a kind of hope that is constantly wanting something. Such hope is a sign of never being satisfied. We are also free of the fear that always attempts to avoid painful situations. These are extreme states. Constantly vacillating between hope and fear creates an unstable and troublesome mind.

In both running and meditation, one needs focus, determination, and a goal. At the same time, that determination and goal can become a disease. We become ambitious and are therefore plagued by hope and fear, which destabilizes our training and practice. Thus the garuda phase is letting go of hope and fear—not as a technique to achieve our goal, but as a genuine recognition that hope and fear stifle our potential and infringe deeply on our mental well-being. They tighten our mind and limit our possibilities. It is just a vicious cycle in which hope is driven by fear, and fear is driven by hope. We cannot allow ourselves to have big dreams because we are plagued by our fears. To break out of this cycle, we must release ourselves from such small-mindedness by relaxing into an even bigger space.

Both hope and fear result from the inability to appreciate

what we have and what we have accomplished. In terms of our meditation practice, in the garuda phase, we develop more intelligence. This kind of insight is known as *prajna*, a Sanskrit word meaning "higher knowledge" or "the best knowledge." We begin to see how the vicious cycle of hope and fear undermines not only our running but also our life. With *prajna*, we can foil our paranoid mind with wisdom, decreasing its propensity to spin off into scenarios of hope and fear. That's how running beyond our conventional limits helps us to expand our mind. We use our garuda runs to work with our mind and catch it before it goes into hope and fear cycles.

Through our meditation sessions, we can address these cycles of hope and fear. When we begin to observe our mind in meditation, we see how much of our psychological energy we put into these two cycles. The practice of overcoming hope is recognizing our positive qualities. With excessive hope, we begin to belittle what we have achieved. We might then feel inadequate and have fear of not achieving more. This fear downgrades our accomplishment and spurs on our hope. Here, "hope" means the feeling of not being good enough. In meditation, when we find ourselves veering into hope, we practice relaxing with who we are and what we have achieved.

We do not move beyond hope and fear by belittling ourselves. Rather, we need to inspire and motivate ourselves. This involves the practice of visualization, which works with the theory that you are what you think. If you visualize something peaceful, you become more peaceful. If you visualize something frightening, you become scared.

We are, in fact, using some form of visualization throughout our whole day. We can feel its effect directly, for if we visualize pizza, we start getting hungry. If we visualize a bear chasing us down the trail, we get scared. So visualization is not that uncommon. In relation to sports, it has become quite standard to visualize your race. Before a race, I like to drive the course. Later, when I am running, in a sense I am running through my visualization.

There is a difference between visualizing and fantasizing. Generally, the best way to use visualization is by visualizing the ideal scenario. So one visualizes the perfect image. If you know you can run a 3:00 marathon, visualizing a 3:10 pace is completely realistic. Visualizing that you are going to run a 2:10 is fantasy.

In using visualization, you have to mimic the possible.

For example, when you do advanced meditation, first you contemplate the qualities of compassion and love, and then you begin to foster them in yourself. By imagining someone you love, you generate a feeling of love and stay with it, becoming familiar with it. As you do that, that love gets ingrained. Later, it will be easier for you to have love.

As a form of visualization practice for running, visualize yourself doing the run, and then actually engage in that run. Rather than re-create yourself, or even improve yourself, use visualization to expand your potential. This is a key lesson from meditation: how to focus on the positive while seeing where and how you can improve. This technique is helpful in addressing fear.

Fear is the result of not wanting to experience something that is unpleasant. Thus we are fearful of the feeling of losing the race, fearful of not accomplishing our goal. Clearly, if our goals are unrealistic, then there is more reason for fear. So addressing our unrealistic hope first relieves our level of fear. Then, experiencing our natural healthiness and respecting who we are—experiencing our feeling of self-worth—is how we undercut fear.

Hope itself is a great trickster. We feel that we are getting closer to what we want, while in fact it is luring us away. This dynamic is very true for the meditator and very real for the runner. Hope always has an illusory object in mind. It is the feeling of propelling ourselves to some future state of being. Thus we see ourselves winning the race. Fear is the result of not having enough wisdom or knowledge. Fear makes us objectify a situation through the eyes of fear, rather than seeing what is actually happening. Fear propels us to knee-jerk reactions.

For athletes, fear is often connected with attachment. We are attached to our body, and therefore we are afraid of losing strength and flexibility or fitness, or of hurting ourselves. Attachment itself does not provide much benefit: essentially, we are just fixating. Whether we are attached or not, our fitness is going to come and go. Compounding that fear by worrying about it does not help.

It is not surprising that runners are attached to their athletic endeavors, just as scholars are attached to their knowledge and status. Scholars feel that knowing what others don't know gives them an edge; athletes feel their fitness gives them the edge. Therefore for athletes to be more attached to the fitness of their bodies is natural. However, such attachment to your physicality can be draining for the mind. It is a level of hope—hanging on to an idealized version of yourself.

The bigger the attachment, the bigger our swings of hope and fear. These hope and fear cycles wreak havoc on the body. After an intense period of training, we may become exhausted from hope. Then we may drop the exercise and start gaining weight, falling into exactly what we had feared. When we have so much hope and fixation, we become exhausted from holding on and have to let go. We then become heavy, less healthy, and out of shape.

A certain amount of hope and fear is most likely inevitable, but when it becomes excessive, it can be destabilizing mentally and physically. Thus, with the garuda's intelligence and accurate assessment, we become more grounded, which gives us the freedom and balance to go beyond hope and fear. Fear is not believing in our basic goodness. Hope is not trusting that it exists. In meditation, hope is the inability to recognize the good qualities of your mind. Fear is not having confidence in the inherent strength of your mind. Therefore hope leads you away from yourself and fear brings things toward you. In this light, hope is not being content with what we have. Fear is not being able to handle what we don't want. Breaking through this cycle is outrageous. That is the gift of the garuda.

29
Spontaneity

We never know what will happen next. The point of being alive is to be there for it. *Spontaneous* means "unplanned and immediate." You cannot really plan a spontaneous activity; it's a matter of being present in the moment and letting it happen.

In the case of running, spontaneity energizes our run. In the case of meditation, spontaneity brings freshness. That is ironic: since we are practicing being present, our meditation should always be inspirational or fresh. However, since we are creatures of habit, we tend to standardize even our spontaneity. Genuine spontaneity serves to remind us of our original purpose.

In building a base, we use routine to build the positive qualities of body and mind—in running, strong bones and muscles, and in meditation, mindfulness and awareness. We need this strong foundation in order to use these activities as a base for fitness, health, peace, and wisdom.

In both meditating and running, we need to be consistent in order to build a base. Yet there is always a fine line between building a base—having discipline and routine—and falling into a rut. Sometimes while pursuing consistency we lose our inspiration. Our spontaneity can evaporate if our running or meditation becomes rote. It could be our routine is running us down. In the practice of meditation this is known as "over-applying the antidote."

Forgetting our purpose is another factor that sabotages our running and our meditation. If we forget why we are doing it, we will no longer feel inspired to run or to sit. Therefore we begin to lose our base. Our body gets out of shape and our mind becomes stressed.

In the garuda phase, even if you do the same run on the same streets at the same time of day with the same people, you run with the mind of spontaneity. You may be inspired to run to a tree in the meadow, or to dart up a new hill. Perhaps you let the other runner choose the route. Even on a treadmill, you can have a spontaneous run, changing the speed or the incline to explore new territory.

Spontaneity can serve to reawaken our purpose. It can shift our momentum to bring energy into what we are doing. It can break us out of our routine and broaden our view. This is how the garuda moves beyond hope and fear.

30
Trails, Hills, and Weather

One of the best things about running in Colorado is trail running on the small dirt pathways that meander through the foothills and mountains. Near Shambhala Mountain Center, there are endless trails where one can run through mountain valleys and up steep ridges, occasionally wading through or jumping across a stream. The Boulder area has one of the most extensive trail systems in the country. Running along these trails is a great harmonizer of mind and body.

Trail running is good for core training, since you have to make minor adjustments and jump over rocks, which is also wonderful for balance. In order not to trip or fall, your attention must be focused and, at the same time, you have to remain relaxed. This is a great way of being present. When you run on trails, you often have to run more slowly, which seems easier on the body. Also, running on dirt has less impact on the body than running on asphalt or concrete. Almost always, there will be hills on a trail. These often reward the runner with a change of scenery at the top or a particularly stunning view.

Even just a slight hill changes the run completely. Immediately our body has to work harder. It can sometimes be quite challenging. My approach to an uphill run is to surrender and, at the same time, to have determination. Especially if it is a large hill, "surrender" doesn't mean just giving up. It means acknowledging that the hill is a force to be reckoned with. I try to respect it rather than pretend it isn't there or fight it all the way up. At the same time, determination is required, for without determination, we feel overwhelmed, and the hill slowly beats us, collapsing our posture and draining our energy.

For the Big Sur Marathon, I had been training on hills, so by the time I got to the race's well-known hill, I was inspired to run up it. Not that it wasn't challenging, but respecting that hill and having determination, my friends and I were able to scale it successfully. The big hill was followed by several more hills during that marathon. For some people, these last hills were daunting, but on that day, we were able to work with them. In fact, they gave us even more determination. As we ran up the final hills, people were cheering us on.

On the other hand, running on a slight downhill, you can often get into a fluid and synchronized pace. Because there is a little momentum, you feel like you are flying. My fellow marathoner Jon Pratt has remarked that when he runs down hills, he feels no self-consciousness. Many runners feel this fluidity and freedom. What we are feeling is the balance and freedom of the garuda.

I have had my fair share of running in extreme weather. If you are a runner, you don't have a choice. Because I am always traveling to different climates, I have run into some incredible temperature variations, from minus 30 to over 115 degrees Fahrenheit. One of my most memorable days was running the Mount Margaret Trail in Colorado.

I had just finished giving a long lecture on meditation and Buddhist philosophy. It was late afternoon, and I thought that I had time for a run. A group of us drove the twenty minutes to Mount Margaret, got out of the car, and started running, noticing that that there was a mass of dark clouds in the north.

As we ran, the clouds came closer, the temperature dropped dramatically, and it started to rain. When we decided to turn around, the massive black cloud came right toward us, raising the bar with some hail and lightning. The closer we got to finishing, the closer the lightning came. We knew we were in trouble when the lightning and thunder started to happen at the same time. But then we encountered a large herd of cows that seemed terrified, mooing and scampering about. By now we had lightning striking all around us, accompanied by horizontal rain. We were being pelted with hail, and we found ourselves surrounded by galloping free-range cows.

Someone said it was good to be running with the cattle because if the lightning were to strike, it would strike them first. That did not seem very compassionate to me, but in times of fear and danger, compassion is often the first thing to go. That's why we practice stabilizing it in meditation. The eeriest thing was that the lightning and the cloud seemed to be following us: when the trail went to the left, the cloud turned left. We were running through a semiforested area, but to get back to the car, we had to sprint across a large open meadow. So we dashed across the meadow, where the lightning could easily strike us, feeling like open targets on a battlefield.

We then did negative splits, running the second half of the trail faster than the first. The cows followed us for a long time, but we eventually had to go our separate ways. Once we got back to the car, lightning struck nearby. We were happy to have survived. Because the weather took us beyond our comfort zone, there was no doubt that we were very present and mindful during that run.

31
Mind Like Sky

On a crisp, fresh morning in the Scottish Highlands, I had planned a ten-mile run. Both Jon Pratt and I were training a lot that winter, and we were both in good shape. Our run had a delightful and magical quality. My mind was very clear, and I remained completely present, noticing every rock on the trail and even the dew glistening on the pine needles. Every gust of wind invigorated and refreshed me. Even the clear echoes of our feet hitting the trail brought me back to the moment. As we inhaled and exhaled, the vapors created a mist. I felt connected to the sky and the earth. My mind was completely there for everything in the environment, yet it remained calm, and I was also self-aware.

In that run, we were experiencing meditation in action. In Tibetan, this is known as *selwa*—"awareness and clarity." When the mind is totally present, it is relaxed, nimble, and sensitive. It feels lighter and clearer. It notices everything, but it is not distracted by anything. It is the feeling of knowing exactly where you are and what you are doing.

We usually think of self-awareness as self-consciousness, which is more of a negative state in which we are focused on ourselves, with a lack of mental expansiveness. We might feel introverted or claustrophobic. That space is not *selwa*: we may be self-aware, but our mind is neither clear nor nimble. In fact, it is in a state of bewilderment. Since our field of vision and mental scope are limited, it is hard to make accurate decisions. We are so self-conscious that we have no perspective on what we are doing. We have no *prajna*.

The clear and knowing meditative self-awareness that Jon and I were experiencing on that day is a result of the mind's being free of baggage, relaxed in its environment, and appreciative. We were understanding our place in the scheme of things—that we are not separate from our environment. We therefore do not want to be anywhere else mentally, because we are genuinely right here. We are not distracted by negative thoughts or daydreaming. The mind is totally in sync with its surroundings. Because it is not comparing this experience to another situation in the past, or wishing for something better in the future, there is no boredom. The exuberance and joy of this state is not necessarily elation; rather, it is a deep feeling of satisfaction. This is the contentment of the tiger, the delight of the lion, and the freedom and balance of the garuda.

What we were experiencing that day was not an alternate universe or some kind of high. It was neither a random occurrence nor a mood. Rather, we were beginning to feel the natural qualities of our own mind—the natural outgrowth of our meditation practice.

Many runners have experienced this level of clarity and precision. For lack of a better term, it is labeled "runner's high." It is commonly assumed that runner's high is physically induced by the release of endorphins. Certainly, when we run and engage in other physical activities, endorphins are released, and we are less sensitive to pain. Likewise, even in the meditation tradition, we use physical exercises to help settle the mind. They work on the principle of cleansing the body of agitation and stress: exhausting the body with movement allows the mind to be more workable. By the same token, having a good long run after work exhausts the body, which directly and indirectly makes the mind more pleasant and workable. There is a direct correlation between physical exertion and mental relief.

The level of clarity that occurs during meditation is not simply the result of physical activity. Rather, clarity is what the mind *is*, like the sky. Stress and agitation are like clouds. If we don't see the sky very often and it suddenly breaks through the clouds, its clarity may feel like an anomaly, but we know it is the sky. Just so, when the practice of meditation lets the natural skylike mind break through the clouds of discursive thought and worry, what we are seeing is the mind's innate clarity, awareness, and joy.

The more familiar we become with that awareness and joy, the more it becomes the continuum of our mind. Similarly, if we ingrain the habit of anxiety and worry, then *that* becomes the continuum of our mind. The difference between stress and clarity is that clarity is inherent, noncreated. No matter how many cloudy days we have, behind the clouds the sky is clear, blue, and bright.

We are like Mother Nature, creating weather by being distracted, irritated, angry, and stressed. We are also like the weather person, constantly talking about it, and how it might change. Like the weather person, who has an intuitive sense of when a storm clears, we also know that when the weather clears, the mind's original clarity and brilliance will appear, and it's going to be a beautiful day. The word *beauty* means "appealing and balanced." This aptly describes the natural quality of our mind.

32

Accurate Assessment

One of the great teachers of meditation, Shantideva, says that beauty is one of the mind's innate qualities. That beauty refers to the mind's having symmetry, like a beautiful flower. Another aspect of beauty is knowledge. On our run, Jon Pratt and I were experiencing those two aspects, not because our surroundings were unusually appealing and balanced, but because the mind had symmetry. It was not overly introverted or extroverted, nor was it lopsided with too many thoughts. The mind and body were in balance. This awareness of internal beauty allowed us to experience external beauty, so we were able to appreciate the trees, the grass, the uneven rocks, and even the sudden gusts of cold wind. This is the bird's-eye view of the garuda.

Recognizing the beauty of our experience is awareness. The word *awareness* means "the knowledge of something." The most beautiful thing to know is that the mind is naturally clear and radiant. This "accurate assessment" or "best knowledge" is called *prajna*. The awareness and insight of *prajna* becomes increasingly important as we continue the meditative journey. Knowing the truth of how things are allows us to endure much hardship. Not knowing what is true—or forgetting about the basic goodness of the mind—frequently derails the meditator. Similarly, forgetting how healthy running is for the body and mind frequently derails many runners. As we ran that day, the awareness and clarity I was experiencing was not unexpected, because I already knew that it was the natural state of my mind. Therefore I could relax within that knowledge, which enabled me to foster the experience.

Knowing the natural state of the mind to be awareness and clarity is the key to applying the mind of meditation to our running and other activities. It is this "best knowledge" that transforms running from a vacillating spectrum of emotional highs and lows to a journey of self-awareness.

How can we foster the accurate assessment of the garuda on the running trail? First of all, we must know where we are and what we are doing. We tend to use running as a way to zone out, taking our mind far away from our physical activity. When that happens, our body and mind have separated. It is not a happy marriage. The body is left in the kitchen doing the dishes while the mind is off in the living room watching television.

When we apply the mind of meditation, as the mind begins to relax into its self-awareness, it is being helped by mindfulness. We have the right balance between too much focus and not enough. Unlike the contained environment of sitting meditation, during the course of an outdoor run we may encounter a new environment every second. Our object of mindfulness may change accordingly, depending on the terrain and how we are feeling. We might first focus on the breath, and then the movement of the feet. Then our focus might move to our visual field: we notice a tree, a rock, or a car. Moving our meditation from one object to another should not be considered distraction. Rather, we are simply changing our focus. We apply enough attention to what we are doing, but we do not force it. In this light, we have a self-awareness of our body moving through space. Visually, we keep our gaze relaxed. There is a constant sense of coming back to where we are. It is the feeling of occupying our mind with what we are doing, without being too critical. Within this comfortable balance, we find the freedom to go farther.

In the garuda phase, the object of our meditation is mindfulness itself. Our attention rests on the experience of the mind being fully present, cognizant, and aware. It is neither unduly withdrawn into itself nor distracted and lured by its focus—the tactile sense of the feet hitting the ground or the visual sense of the fog in front of the trees. Rather, the mind feels full and within itself. When this occurs, there is little discursive thinking. The mind is not distracted, but present.

In one regard, emphasizing mindfulness is an advanced technique: we are using the power of our mind to guide the mind. However, it also feels easy to be present in the course of running because in so many ways, running encourages us to be mindful. Therefore I believe that this mindfulsness technique is natural and enjoyable for the running meditator.

In order to use mindfulness as an object, the running meditator needs to have some understanding and experience of how mindfulness feels. We discover this first in meditation. Through continued awareness of mindfulness in meditation and in running, this practice can become a steady guide, like the horizon or a distant star, and we can remain mindful and present throughout a run.

The technique of using mindfulness as your focus is dependent upon being comfortable in your running environment. Just as in sitting meditation, when you are comfortable, you can more readily bring your focus back to the breath or a contemplation. If you're constantly distracted, it is very difficult to achieve depth in meditation. Likewise, if you are continuously uncomfortable with your environment, it will be very difficult for you to experience a deeper level of the running mind. With cars, rain, hail, wind, or pedestrians, you may be constantly distracted. When the run is over, your mind might feel more frenzied. In a more supportive environment—running next to a river or on a quiet street—you will naturally go to a deeper level of consciousness.

The key to this meditation is knowing what mindfulness is. Once meditation has brought confidence to your mind, you will be able to practice mindfulness in almost any circumstance. You will feel a certain equanimity even in challenging environments. When you are neither threatened nor seduced by external distractions, you can naturally relax almost anywhere, resting in a deeper consciousness and a more mindful mind, because you are fully present.

Finding the place where we are comfortably balanced alleviates the boredom of running, which is often the result of a lack of self-respect and too much comparing. Boredom has an interest scale, and it correlates directly with self-worth. We don't consider our activity worthy of our attention, and therefore we're not that interested. Sometimes boredom is related to pride. For example, when we consider an activity like waiting for the bus as beneath us, we become irritated or angry.

In running with mind of meditation, we are taking the attitude that our experience is worthy of our attention. When we think an activity is worthy, we do not start to compare it to other experiences. When we start comparing an activity to our memories of the past or our fantasies of the future, that means we think it could be better, so we are downgrading it further. When we are in a good mood and we appreciate what we are doing—running in the gym or going for a run in a not-so-scenic place—those runs become enjoyable and meaningful because we are present for them. Appreciation and self-worth are therefore good qualities for competitive runners to cultivate as alternatives to the fuel of ambition. They have the capacity to take us farther down the road.

One of the benefits of the outrageous runs is that we run without ambition. Since running is essentially a goal-driven sport, at this phase of running, we can relieve ourselves of that orientation. Part of what allows us to be goalless in this phase is an inherent trust in our fitness and our ability. We do not have to prove ourselves. At this level, it does not actually matter. We have achieved so many goals in the past that now the only goal is no goal. Mentally, the garuda phase means running without hope and fear, not running by constantly being driven. Running in this way helps us to be more present.

When ambition is our main motivation, it throws us out of balance. Running on self-worth completely eliminates the need to become overly arrogant and put others down when they aren't running on our level. We save energy this way. Self-worth even allows us to appreciate the talents of other athletes without feeling threatened by them.

As we become more and more familiar with our own experience of running, and therefore how our mind feels, we are ingraining that ability to be present, clear, and knowing. Maintaining a balanced, meditative space on our run, we are able to relax and make an accurate assessment of what we're doing. That is the practice of the garuda.

33

Too Far Out

During the outrageous phase, we need to be careful about not getting too far out. The secret of the garuda is that its outrageousness is completely dependent on our being grounded. We must not turn into Icarus, flying too close to the sun and melting our wings. Running too far or becoming emotionally or socially unavailable can definitely be an obstacle, for in so doing, we are becoming ungrounded. We may become isolated from our family and friends.

Similarly in meditation, if we are too isolated, too much in our head and in our thoughts, the energy shifts. We refer to these extreme states of mind as "temporary states," because they are characterized by the illusion that we are making progress, when we are actually in the throes of a mild hallucination, not a meditative realization. We meditate to become more healthy, available, compassionate, and present. If we find ourselves less healthy, available, compassionate, or present, then we are missing the point. Similarly, if we run too much, we may become depleted and emaciated. Before, we were building ourselves up, but now we are tearing ourselves down.

These "ungrounding" experiences result from a number of factors, but often they stem from a subtle level of pride. We feel we are efficient runners or meditators: we know the ropes, so we begin to pay less attention to the basics. As always, this tinge of pride slowly begins to blow us off course. In meditation, we start wanting to experience things that others have not. Rather than letting experiences naturally arise, we try to foster ultimate states of mind. We become disenfranchised from genuine meditation practice because we can't perceive what is actually happening. Communication becomes difficult because pride has isolated us.

The way to overcome this obstacle is to reground ourselves with the basic techniques of mindfulness and awareness. We may want to reacquaint ourselves with the motivation behind our meditation or our running. We may even want to go to a more experienced runner or meditation practitioner to give us some guidance. If we are running a lot, or meditating a lot, we must always be mindful of these potential obstacles.

Mindfulness and awareness allow us to experience the freedom and space of the run. So much of our modern world is structured, but running does not have to be just one more obligation. Especially in the garuda phase, we have achieved many of our goals. Having more goals only complicates matters. Now is the time for relaxation. We are running simply because we love it, not because it is a long run, or because we are doing intervals, but because to run is the only ambition that we have. Like children giddy with summer, we are running because it feels good.

Even if you are an advanced runner and a proficient meditator, remember that the qualities of the tiger and the lion keep the garuda in touch with earth. On these long and adventurous runs, try to maintain your attention all the way to the end—both mindfulness and awareness, both introspection and consciousness. Even when you are challenging yourself in new territory, remaining focused, aware, and relaxed is the baseline approach. You may even have a slight level of fear because you do not know the area. Obviously, you should be careful. Don't do potentially dangerous runs, but make them challenging. At the same time, keep your bird's-eye view in play, joining mindfulness and awareness to make an accurate assessment of conditions—without getting too far out.

GARUDA CONTEMPLATION: LOVE AND KINDNESS

In the garuda phase, we expand our mind to include others. Happiness is the experience of love and kindness between family and friends. The thought of love is the most powerful of feelings. The love of our parents is what brings us here, and our mother's love especially enables us to survive. The love of one human being for another allows us to communicate and grow. The less intense version of love is kindness. Expressing love and kindness to others benefits them and roots us in our own happiness. This love and kindness is innate in the human mind and heart. Even though most of us experience it in random moments, it is something we can cultivate. Like the freedom of the garuda, it is measureless and limitless.

The way to begin the meditation on love and kindness is by bringing to mind someone you love. When you think about that person, a feeling of kindness, affection, and love arises. Love grows when you feel a wish for another to be happy. It may not be a deep emotional upwelling, but this innate altruistic moment takes the mental spotlight off yourself and shines it on others when you think of what would make them happy. Once you've aroused that feeling, stay with it. This is very powerful practice because it can overcome our selfishness. And, ironically, the feeling of love and concern for others is the best way to make ourselves happy.

Over the centuries, meditators have determined that the root of unhappiness, suffering, and stress is essentially self-centeredness. As we do this contemplation, of course we continue to take good care of ourselves, but our attitude has shifted from looking at the world with the question, What will make me happy? When we expect external circumstances to bring happiness, we are setting ourselves up for one disappointment after another. The garuda flies beyond such conventionality and small-mindedness.

The contemplation at the garuda stage consists mainly of the deep wish for others to be happy. After settling our posture and calming our mind, we place our focus on love and kindness. First we think of our friends and family and extend to them our heartfelt love and kindness. Then we visualize the limitless force of those qualities reaching even distant friends and acquaintances. Then we extend it to people we do not know. As we do this, we realize that love is infinitely expandable. Our heart and mind are actually growing larger as we practice. Now we extend love and kindness even to our enemies and other difficult people. This is how we train the innate capacity of our mind and heart.

The contemplation on compassion involves bringing someone to mind who is in pain. Immediately we feel some empathy. We wish for this person's discomfort and pain to stop. That thought is compassion. In this contemplation, we become familiar with compassion, we develop it, and we train ourselves in it. In this way, a compassionate attitude becomes more natural.

The benefit of contemplating love and compassion is that it allows us to express these virtues more readily in our life. These contemplations are a very powerful way to make the mind stronger and more resilient, and also to make us happy. They enable us to accommodate more with our mind, making the fabric of the mind stronger. Our mind thus becomes less stressed and less taxed by daily activity.

Love and compassion are elements that need to be exercised

by the mind. If we exercise unkindness and anger, we only become better at it. In this state, we go from irritation to disregard
and animosity. These emotions do not feel good. They weigh
heavily on our mind, and we feel worn out, if not exhausted.
These contemplations on love and compassion are training the
mind to go in another direction—beyond thinking only of our
own fitness and well-being.

PART V

DRAGON

34
The Dragon

Running and meditation both have a secretive and mysterious quality that is beyond words. The dragon embodies this feeling of deep purpose—beyond expression and only to be experienced. Within this phase, we contemplate deep and powerful themes. They are our personal secrets—thoughts, feelings and insights—that are so intimate they cannot be properly expressed or understood by others. This secret inner level gives human beings depth.

The dragon phase is where the magnanimity of our being begins to truly shine. By training our mind and body through running and meditation, we have become strong, gentle, and kind. Now we have reached a personal and social crossroads. Our running and our meditation have undergone a great transformation. No longer are these activities solely for our personal benefit; we use our solitary endeavors to benefit others. Our running can become a tool to benefit the world.

The intention to use our activity to benefit others is elusive and mysterious, like the dragon itself. But as running meditators we know that when we are brave enough to be in the present, we have the power to transform the world. The dragon embodies all the lessons of the tiger, lion, and garuda—mindful, perky, and in balance. Thus the dragon arises as coincidence and auspiciousness. In this phase, the running meditator comes to terms with this dynamism: the mysterious and mystical dragon is a symbol of the inexpressible power, brilliance, and profundity of the human mind.

In the Shambhala tradition, the dragon acknowledges that moment when the warrior's mind moves toward nonconceptual wisdom. When this unique feeling of complete embodiment and transcendence occurs, we call it the joining of earth and heaven. There is a deep sense of honesty, both personally and socially. Ironically, touching this inexpressibility connects us to others in a magical way.

The dragon is a symbol of this paradox. It is said to live on the ground, but it also flies high among the clouds, moving and shifting, peeking out, then feinting back into plumes of cumulus whiteness.

In the West, the dragon is the creature slain by Saint George, and it can represent danger. In the East, it is highly venerated for its power, magic, and auspiciousness. In Tibet, I heard various stories about people seeing this mysterious creature. The kingdom of Bhutan, which is nestled between India and China, is known in Tibetan as *drukyul,* "the land of dragons." In China, the dragon is the ultimate symbol of wisdom. It was used as a sign of the emperors, representing the principle of heaven, which is characterized by power and benevolence. If the emperor ruled wisely, heaven and earth would be joined, and peace and prosperity would reign. The dragon is therefore known as inscrutable.

For runners and meditators, the dragon represents the mysterious phase in which we develop a level of insight that allows us to connect with our deep inner wishes and aspirations. On these contemplative runs, we are not just indulging in day-dreaming or fantasies or blowing off mental steam. Rather, we are bringing beneficial thoughts to mind. In a dragon run, we focus on connecting with the important themes that are running throughout our life. The run becomes the meditation as we focus on a chosen thought.

The most beneficial thoughts are those of compassion, caring for others, or thinking beyond just ourselves. This focus can be challenging to runners because running is such an individual sport. It can also be overly self-engrossing. But there are other kinds of beneficial thoughts you can focus on. For example, if you decide you want to make a change in your life, running and contemplating may help you see how to make that change.

Moving the body and bringing up an important thought to contemplate are highly compatible activities. We might become aware that we have made a mistake and that we need to apologize to somebody. We might contemplate the direction that our life is taking. We might ponder aspects of our life that we want to change. We might review our aspirations and dreams. For example, we might see ourselves running toward what we want to accomplish.

In the ancient meditation texts, the distinction between being wise and being foolish is not so much who you are but how you utilize what you have. Wise people have imagination. No matter what confronts them, they are able to see possibility. When presented with the same circumstance, the fool has no imagination, so there are no possibilities. I find this bit of wisdom helpful in running, meditation, and life in general.

In reality, sometimes we are foolish and sometimes we are

wise. When life presents challenges and we are able to utilize them, we are wise. When we become overwhelmed and see no possibilities, we become foolish.

When we are wise in meditation, we are able to keep each moment fresh. But once we begin to lose our imagination, apathy's arrow strikes us. Likewise, in running, if we lose our imagination we are struck by the arrow of slothfulness.

Ultimately, life is a process of developing the ability to always see how to utilize what is in front of us. Since the mind is infinite and possibilities are infinite, if we succumb to the view that something is impossible, we have given in to thinking there is only one possibility.

Being imaginative should not be confused with being aggressive. It does not mean simply pushing ahead. It means being able to look at what is happening from a panoramic, 360-degree view. Being aggressive, however, is forcing one dimension of reality.

Therefore in the long journey of life we are constantly faced with different scenarios. In this light we must look at each daily run and the imagination it requires. Even if we are injured we must be imaginative to find different ways of exercising. Likewise, if we are meditating, we must find different ways to be mindful. If our schedule is busy, we must still find ways to train our mind. This is an essential quality of the dragon—being able to see life's possibilities.

Finding a comfortable spot in which to meditate for a few minutes, even if it is in the middle of our run, can help us physically, in terms of exercise, and also mentally, in terms of clarifying what is important. Confidence we get from the run might also give us the courage to apologize, change jobs, or realize that some of our habits are eroding our personal integrity.

We might see how these habits are grounded in attachment, fear, or self-obsession.

In the dragon phase, you might run at a slower pace, which allows you to look at inner feelings, thoughts, and insights that you might want to consider deeply. That may mean running in solitude on a secluded trail, or rising very early in the morning to run alone. One of my favorite dragon runs is a particular nine-mile loop in Colorado. About halfway through, I pass a small lake that ends in a meadow. The edge of the meadow drops off into a valley, offering a great vista.

The dragon is often associated with auspiciousness. One day, I decided to go to my secret dragon running spot. I was contemplating certain changes that I wanted to make. In the Tibetan tradition, we often look for signs. For example, if you see a bowl of fruit, it represents something positive happening, or if you see a broken branch, that might represent some negativity. On that day, when I came to the meadow, there was a white horse. Though I had never before seen any horses in that field, there it stood, staring at me. It galloped in a circle, which took my breath away. Then, as I gazed down into the valley in meditation, the horse stood there, gazing back at me. This I took to be a positive sign.

Auspiciousness might sound like a superstition. However, we live in this world, and we are constantly in an exchange with it, whether or not we know it. When we begin to appreciate the world and learn to be more observant of what is happening, instead of being purely self-centered, we begin to see these signs.

During this phase, no one needs to know what we are contemplating. Some aspects of our life we share, and others we keep to ourselves. This level of mystery brings balance to our being. If everyone knows everything about us, a certain dignity and mystery is lost. If we are too secretive, a certain availability is lost.

Thus the dragon is beneficial not only for our running but also for our life and the world—bestowing wisdom, inspiration, and inscrutability.

35
The Dragon's Breath

In both running and meditating, we become very familiar with the breathing process. In the beginning it is hard to find—and hard to stay with—the breath. The technique may even seem overwhelming. Like a great chef, however, with progress one becomes a master of subtlety. As we become attuned—mindful and sophisticated—we can taste how our breath feels. It is no longer simply air rushing in and out of our body; now it has texture. Some days it is rough and slightly coarse or choppy. On others it is smooth, gliding in and out like spring water or silk. The breath is sweet, delicious, and alluring, and sometimes bitter, with a bite. At times it is gentle and almost invisible.

All these textures are the result of conditions—from how we feel to what we eat, from whom we see to how our day is going. Because it is life itself, the breath has tremendous power to communicate. Meditation and mindfulness allow us the subtlety required to delineate the qualities of the breath. In this way, meditating on the breath is like a mirror into our mind and our life.

Through that moment of relating to the breath, we learn how we are leading our life. No matter how the breath feels in its texture, we should appreciate it. Rough or coarse breath can reflect that we are tired and overworked, or that there is some conflict or obstacle in our life. This may stem from how we are behaving. As well, if we are too aggressive in applying the meditative technique, our winds may be disturbed. We must therefore be more gentle. Breath that is more gentle might indicate harmony, relaxation, or other positive feelings.

Relatively speaking, meditation relaxes or calms us down and gives us a chance to be aware of what arises, which can be connected to the breath as well as to greater life issues. If fear arises, it might indicate that we are crowding our breath and focusing too much on the inhalation. If we are unfocused and spacey, it may indicate that we are too nonchalant with the breath, overemphasizing exhalation. As meditators, we learn to adjust. When the mind is bombarded with myriad thoughts, they stem not from meditation, but from life. Our reaction—guilt or anger, for example—may point us toward examining particular aspects of our life more carefully. In this way, the breath can be a guide for living.

Generally, there are two approaches to breathing meditation: one more gentle and consistent and the other more coarse. The gentle level of breathing is inherent in various kinds of sitting meditation in which our body is not moving a great deal. The coarse breathing meditation is related to vigorous exercise and requires more control. In this light, running generally deals with the coarse level of breathing. When using coarse or forceful breathing, the mind tends to become stimulated and distracted. Therefore this practice takes a meditator who has strong mindfulness.

At the same time, running can also promote a gentle quality in the breath, which allows for a deeper level of contemplation. In general, breathing hard while running stimulates the thinking process, but it can also exhaust the mind.

When I was visiting Tibet, I had a vivid experience of

dealing with the breath. I had been there for many weeks and had not had the opportunity to go running. Because of my role as a spiritual leader, anytime I ventured out of the monastery, a monk holding incense would lead the way while other monks played Tibetan horns—the customary procession in Tibet. During my time there, I conducted a variety of ceremonies: blessing the ill, blessing the children, and opening a school. At other times I conducted ceremonies composed of elaborate rituals that often included blessing thousands of people. These rituals could easily take all day, and even preparing for them would take several hours. Thus my time was limited. Being on a tight schedule and constantly surrounded by people in a very formal environment, I was unable to get outside for runs.

One morning I woke up early to see if it was possible for me to actually go for a run in Tibet. But there were a few challenges before the run began. The first was to get out of the monastery and find a secluded area where I would not be seen. Next, I would have to change from my Tibetan robes into more fitting attire for running. Not least, could I even run at this altitude, where even the valley bottoms are thirteen thousand feet above sea level?

I asked Ted Rose, one of the few runners on the trip, to accompany me. We left the monastery by jeep. After driving for a while, we found a stretch of land between two remote villages. I changed out of my lama robes and put on my running clothes, and we headed down the valley. It was delightful to get out for a run after so much ceremonial activity; I felt completely privileged and shocked by the opportunity to run on the roof of the world. We passed grazing yaks and appreciated the stunning scenery. Then suddenly I had a strange feeling. I was not particularly winded, but at that moment I realized my body was running out of oxygen. We decided to turn back to the jeep and move at a slower pace. At the jeep I changed my clothes, and we headed back to the monastery.

While running at that altitude, I was experiencing a lack of oxygen. That afternoon, I became very tired. In fact, I had to sleep. However, after a good rest, I felt better. I had personally experienced the importance of the breath and how we relate to it. Whether we are breathing the refined air of Tibet or the morning air of India's jungle, our breath plays a critical role in how we experience life. Through running and meditation, we can appreciate this most precious of gifts.

36
What Is the Mind?

n the West, when we talk about our mind, we point to our head, considering the mind to be synonymous with the brain. But in Tibet and other meditative cultures, when asked about their mind, people often place their hand on their chest in the heart area. In fact, no one knows exactly where the mind exists. Like the dragon, it is elusive.

East or West, our general experience of the mind is very personal and intimate: it is how we feel on a given day, or what we think. It is our personal collection of memories and ideas. The English language is somewhat limited in terms of how to even describe the mind: we use the words *mind, consciousness, intellect.* However, in meditative languages like Sanskrit and Tibetan, there are innumerable names for the mind.

Sem is the Tibetan word for the cognitive mind that is based upon subject and object. There is also the word *lo,* which refers to the intellect—what one understands. There is also *yi,* another word used for the conventional cognitive mind. The word *rikpa* means "awareness." This awareness has two meanings: general awareness and nonconceptual awareness, which is linked to the word *wisdom.* Then there is the word *namshi,* which means consciousness. There are said to be eight different levels of consciousness. A variety of other words are used to indicate the enlightened mind, the transcendent mind, or transcendent intelligence.

We can divide these descriptions into two categories. One is the conventional mind of subject and object: you see a house and your mind thinks "house." This is the dualistic mind. The transcendent mind is beyond subject and object: it transcends confusion and duality. It is sometimes referred to as "clear-light mind," "luminosity," "wisdom," or "awakenment."

The conventional mind is said to have characteristics—including the characteristics of clarity and knowing. If humans are made of flesh and bone, and trees are made of wood, the fabric of the conventional mind is said to be that of clarity and knowing. Through the practice of meditation, we begin to experience clarity and knowing. As clarity and knowing expand, in turn they lead us to the transcendent state of being.

Once aware of it, we can experience this awakened mind in all our activities: running, traveling, relating with our friends and family, and eating. Sometimes the mind is coarse, and therefore we experience it as heavy emotion—elation or depression. But its basic goodness is always there, in all of us. Through meditation and the knowledge of what we are doing in meditation, we can discover this mind in ourselves and others.

37
The Power of Intention

am often asked why I run. Mostly it is non-runners who ask, but I understand the question. There are those who find it perplexing that someone in my position would engage in such a sport as running.

Like many people who run, I run for health as well as joy. Running is like flying—there is freedom and levity. We are moving through space above the ground. It is a great way to connect with nature and to breathe fresh air.

There is a deeper meaning, which has to do with my intention. I believe that with pure intention, you can bring almost any activity onto your spiritual path. My intention in running is to benefit others. Thus running is a continuation of my spiritual journey.

Through my years of contemplating the rich spiritual tradition from which I descend, I have learned the potency of intention, which demonstrates the power of the mind. With a powerful mind, if we intend our run to be for the welfare of others, then it is. Conversely, if we turn our meditation into a completely selfish pursuit, that is exactly what it will be. In either activity it is our own intention that determines whether the result is ordinary or extraordinary.

The power of the dragon is intention. The dragon knows that with full, unbridled intention we can bring goodness and benefit into any activity. This means our run can be a powerful incubator of intent. Having the intention to run for the benefit of others changes the fabric of our consciousness. Such a noble, vast intention brings our mind and body strength. It gives character to our being. Our run is no longer centered just on staying in shape or making it to the finish. Rather, it becomes a process of actively training our intention to benefit others in the world.

Having such intention adds dignity to our run. We are no longer just one person running along a trail, in the countryside, or on the street. Our mind and heart are extending further—even globally. In one run, we are contemplating all beings and how we can help the universe.

When we contemplate like this, we should not be constricted by thought, wondering, "What can one person really do?" Rather than worry about specific outcomes, we need to focus on developing our intention. In reality, most ideas that have helped the world have come through intention. The Buddha sat under a tree. Jesus walked in the desert. The Taoist sage Lao-tzu sat in the forest. All these beings had powerful ways to develop their intention. Through that intention they were able to help the world.

We too can take a solitary and lonely activity and turn it into a dynamic period of developing our intention to help the world. Developing such an intention through running can be a joyful and liberating exercise; we automatically become stronger, more able to help others. As well, from such strong intention, ideas and inspiration will no doubt follow.

It is up to us how we would like to use our run. But we should know that as human beings, we have this great secret known as intention.

DRAGON CONTEMPLATION: COMPASSION AND SELFLESSNESS

The contemplation for the dragon is egolessness, going beyond the limitations of self. When our ego gets involved, we lose perspective. We fail to consider how othes are feeling. In this contemplation we discover how to not get in our own way. As always, it is important to remember that we are not making ourselves insignificant or belittling ourselves. Contemplating how we can be a little more selfless makes more room for family and friends in our mind and heart. This is a deep meditation in which we reflect on how we are always putting ourselves first, spoiling many situations as a result. How can we be a little more selfless?

Through sports, we can get an inflated sense of our ego. In this contemplation we let go of that tendency. When we think we've had a bad day, it is often our ego that has taken a beating. If there is less ego, there is less to be batted around. So now we contemplate that we are not our house, our job, our clothing. We are not even necessarily our body or our own fitness. In this way we develop humbleness and softness.

If we practice the dragon contemplation regularly, we will begin to see that the self is essentially an illusion. This mirage-like self is always shifting and changing, but it is never really there. The profound discovery that is made by the dragon meditator is that there is no ego for there to be less of. You cannot lose what you never had.

This meditation therefore often occurs in two stages. In the first stage, we reflect on ways to be less ego centered. In the second, deeper contemplation, we reflect that the self is an illusion.

PART VI

WINDHORSE

38
Conversation

I was in the green hills of Vermont for my annual teaching at Karmê Chöling, a Shambhala center located in a region called the Northeast Kingdom, a picturesque landscape of rolling hills dotted with cows and the occasional dog. After a day of teachings, interviews, and meetings, I needed to relate to my body. I thought to myself, "What better way to end this day than with a nice, long run?"

My companion on that day was Nick Trautz, a quiet, gentle, and extremely fit young man who has been a professional cross-country skier. I always teased Nick that he never seemed to train very much for our runs—it seemed to me he relied mostly on the fitness he acquired through skiing. When he joined me for the Toronto Waterfront Marathon, he had only begun training ten days before. He was definitely in pain after the race, but he did make it to the finish line.

Often when we ran together we did not talk a great deal. But on this particular run, as we slowly meandered through the hills of Vermont in the latter part of the day, we engaged in what I like to consider the art of conversation. We simply enjoyed each other's company. There was no particular subject at hand and no particular point to the conversation. Rather, we used conversation as a way of expressing our friendship.

We were relaxed, sometimes telling stories and sometimes

joking, sharing feelings and insights. Occasionally I would ask Nick how his skiing was going, or he would ask me how traveling and teaching were going. At other times there was silence. There was no awkwardness and no particular need to speak. When we did not speak, the space in the run opened up. At the same time we remained completely purposeful on our run, which ended up being twenty miles long that day. At the end, we both remarked on how natural and effortless it felt. Nick said that it was one of his most enjoyable runs, and I felt the same way.

Running is a time when we can unwind and be with friends. Conversation is a natural and integral part of that experience. We can talk about important themes in our life or simply discuss the weather or how our running is going. Conversation transforms running from a solitary sport to a communal sport. By extension, conversation is integral to human society.

Conversation is different from having a discussion or bringing up talking points. Rather, it is the expression of our innate humanity. The words we speak are the sound of that joy, kindness, and love. In that light, it doesn't really matter what we talk about. In fact, there does not even have to be a point.

It seems that in combining conversation with running, people are more honest with their feelings. That may be because we are in motion. Swinging our legs and arms, and, particularly, inhaling and exhaling, relaxes our uptight and conceptual mind and our social persona. It allows us to be more free and spirited in our expression. As well, it seems much more difficult to tell a lie while we are running, and if we do, we have to work much harder at it. This is all a result of constantly experiencing the breath. The breath is a truth serum of sorts—an expression of honesty regarding how we feel and what we are doing.

Often when we are having a conversation while running,

we feel more receptive. The exchange of ideas and thoughts flows freely. In fact, utilized in the right way, conversation while running can stimulate our brain to help us understand themes that we many not have comprehended previously. Long walks have been known to stimulate the imagination of writers. Perhaps for runners, long runs have the same effect. Even though it may not be a time of deep contemplation, it may help us to understand wisdom we had not seen previously. While we were talking on our runs, Nick would often say, "Oh, I didn't realize that before."

Communication with another individual transforms conversation from the act of saying anything that pops into our head into an art. The art of conversation is not just one person talking incessantly throughout the run but rather a harmonious flow of feelings, thoughts, and ideas. This is why conversation can be a part of a windhorse run (see chapter 40). It is communication, as opposed to an exchange of subject matter or just crowding the space with words. As the old adage goes, the only thing that gets more exercise than the runner's legs is the runner's mouth.

In this light, conversation does not necessarily need to occur. There are times when silence is appropriate—just as knowing when to rest is as important as knowing when to train. For example, you may be ready to have a conversation but your partner is not. We must therefore be sensitive and artful. Certain topics may be painful or inappropriate. To be good at conversation, we must use our sensitivity and perception of the other person, the time, and the space.

The art of conversation is very much alive and well in the Tibetan culture. Because it is appreciated as a form of intelligence and kindness, simple conversations about the tea we are drinking or what the weather is like are not considered to be trivial or superficial. As we talk about these simple subjects, we actually gain a lot of insight into the other person.

Being bicultural, I often find that the Tibetan approach to conversation contrasts in an interesting way with the Western culture. In the West, sometimes conversation is synonymous with bluntness—every topic has to have a fact or a purpose. Being blunt does not always tell others very much. However, there are times when it is appropriate to be straightforward.

The art of conversation is not about being coy or mischievous. It is not a trickery of words or deception. Rather, it is an opportunity for genuine exchange. In our modern culture, the most common opportunity for conversation is when two people are on their first date. We learn a tremendous amount about our partner by engaging in the dance of conversation.

As a running meditator in the phases of the tiger, lion, and garuda, we may be working on the technique of mindfulness and awareness. At the same time, we may be engaged in conversation. Even though some runs may best be served by silence, other runs can provide a container for human friendship and communication. This communal and social expression is an opportunity to share in the basic goodness of humanity.

39
Peace Run

n autumn 2006, His Holiness the Dalai Lama of Tibet consecrated the Great Stupa of Dharmakaya in Colorado as a monument of peace. The stupa sits in the upper part of a valley at the Shambhala Mountain Center, near Red Feather Lakes. It took us fifteen years to build this sacred temple, using the traditional specifications for its bell-shaped body, which is modeled after the sitting Buddha and represents enlightenment. The stupa is crowned with a sun and moon, symbolizing wisdom and compassion. Visitors from all cultures and all faiths arrive daily; children's groups and elderly groups tour the Great Stupa.

One day it occurred to me that it would be fitting to host a peace race that would end at the stupa. For the first Stupa Peace Run, 150 runners turned out, some very advanced and others just beginners. More than a race per se, it was an adventure and celebration.

I wasn't sure if I would run that day, since I was still recovering from an injury. But on the morning of the race I felt better, and it was for a good cause. So I put on my running shoes and joined everyone. Jon Pratt and a few others had organized the event. We gathered in Red Feather Lakes for two events—a 5K and a 15K.

I was moved to see so many runners make the effort to be

there. A few had attended a "Running with the Mind of Meditation" workshop. The Peace Run had attracted a unique blend of people—some who had just come for the run, some runners who had taken up meditation, and some meditators who had taken up running.

Everyone was excited. For some of the runners, it was going to be a challenge, as the run began at 7,500 feet. The sun was shining. I encouraged everyone to take care of themselves and to keep the spirit of the day in mind—that we were running for peace.

The gun went off, and we started running. It was quite amazing to see all the people running through the high country of Colorado for peace. We ran through beautiful meadows, over rocky crevasses, and down toward a stream, entering Shambhala Mountain Center at the final incline toward the stupa. Coming up the valley and seeing this beautiful sacred structure was an incredible way to end a race. I asked people to walk around it, which is customary, rather than run around it, which is not appropriate. My wife, Khandro Tseyang, was waiting to hand out the prizes. She gave everyone a *kata*, the traditional white scarf Tibetans offer in a gesture of friendship, blessing, and auspiciousness.

I felt very moved to see the worlds of running and meditation come together. These two very different groups that I have come to know so well do not usually mix. However, on that day, we had all come together to run for peace, both as meditators and as runners.

40
Windhorse

Running has been extremely rewarding for me personally. But what has made it truly fulfilling is being able to help others through my activity. Not only has my enthusiasm allowed me to connect with others, I also have been able to encourage people to work with their body as well as their mind. On a bigger scale, through marathoning, I have been able to raise funds, merit, and spirit for charities, working mostly toward rebuilding the cultural and spiritual education of Tibet. Initially, I focused on rebuilding the monastery in the Surmang region of eastern Tibet where my father had been abbot, bolstering the inspiration of the local people. I began other humanitarian projects as well.

When I began running, I was not thinking of how it could lead to charitable work, but this has been a natural outgrowth. As we become more fit and confident, we want to share that goodness with others. It has been amazing to see an individual sport like running become so beneficial. The majority of races encourage giving in one form or another. I feel very fortunate to be a part of this charity work, which is a clear sign of the goodwill of humanity.

Running has allowed me to connect with the inherent goodness and healthiness of humanity. I believe this inexpressible feeling of goodness is a critical element in the future of humanity, and that we can create a society based upon our innate basic goodness. In the Shambhala tradition, this is known as "enlightened society." It is based on discovering the inherent goodness that underlies the heart of humanity, even when terrible things happen.

Through running and meditating, we become better citizens of the world. Our appreciation, discipline, and energy benefit a much wider circle. These qualities are fuel for windhorse, the heart of the final phase of training. The Tibetan word is *lungta*. *Lung* means "wind," and *ta* means "horse." Windhorse is the life force energy that naturally arises when we train on the path of tiger, lion, garuda, and dragon. The wind represents the complete awakenment of the human mind. The horse represents expedience, success, and swiftness.

In Tibet, the *lungta* are drawn on prayer flags. These flags are then taken high up on a mountain to flutter in the wind. The windhorse is often painted carrying a jewel on its back, which is known as the wish-fulfilling jewel. This jewel represents the enlightened mind that is capable of anything. It is the source of happiness. What brings true happiness is helping others. This final phase of training, therefore, is deciding to do something beneficial for society. In this way, the spirit of running can be shared with the world. The aggression and speed of our time increase humanity's tendency to lose heart. Whatever any of us can do to swing the tide toward goodness and understanding will help. For example, Mike Sandrock, the running writer, operates One World Running, a nonprofit that sends shoes to underdeveloped countries.

Runners are generally optimistic, and this optimism is what the world needs, for we are constantly told that something is wrong, or about to go wrong, in the world. Runners intuitively know that through dedication and hard work, success can come about: if we, as humanity, dedicate ourselves to creating a better world, then it is completely doable. That is the energy of windhorse. The world as a whole is like one mind. If that giant mind begins to doubt itself and get depressed, our entire planet will be in jeopardy. However, if the collective world conscience develops an ethos of optimism and exertion, we really will have a chance to pull ourselves out of our predicament, because the human race will have windhorse.

My work gives me the opportunity to travel around the world. Year by year, I am struck by the blatant interdependence that connects us all. When I began to study at Namdroling Monastery in southern India, near Bangalore, very few of my North American students had any idea where Bangalore was. Now those same people are having their calls routed through the local call centers there.

The windhorse phase is realizing that we are all gifted; we all have something to offer. Whether it is working with the environment, with children, or at business—all these gifts create windhorse: energy that is moving us in the right direction. In these times, what we do matters, regardless of how insignificant it is. But that is not the point. The point is that we are all optimistic and engaged. In that way, not only is our activity of benefit to others, it is also personally satisfying and leads to contentment and happiness. This is a win-win situation.

One of the great sayings in meditation is that we are perfect, but we need a slight adjustment. That slight adjustment comes down to having confidence in our basic goodness.

In the windhorse contemplation, we contemplate our basic goodness. When all the plans, worrying, and speed dissolve, when we are just sitting there feeling a deep sense of space and well-being, we are resting in the indescribable feeling of basic goodness. It is "basic" in that this is fundamentally who we are. It is "good" in that we are complete, intact, and whole.

An amazing thing about being human is that we can connect with that long-forgotten goodness that we have. It is very powerful to feel that sense of goodness: having confidence and bravery in our innermost being. Even a few moments of sitting and feeling it is healing. After feeling it in ourselves, we begin to see it in everyone and everything. We can see it in a small child. We can see it in an old person. We can see it in a beautiful mountain. We can feel it when we hug someone.

Part of this message of running with the mind of meditation is that we can no longer split spirituality and everyday life. No matter what we are doing, we have the ability to be awake and to live up to our potential. We can run with that energy of basic goodness. When we feel it, we will run stronger—and maybe even faster—but we will certainly feel better. Basic goodness is the wish-fulfilling jewel.

Epilogue

Over a six-year period, I ran nine full marathons and one half marathon. In that time, I learned a great deal about racing.

My first race was the Toronto Marathon. The weather was cold, and my main objective was finishing. It was a challenging and rewarding experience, for I had never run so far in my life. The next marathon was the Big Sur Marathon, which goes along the coastal hills of California on Highway 1. It was a beautiful day, and I ran strong, finishing in a time of 3:21.

The next race was the Edmonton Centennial Marathon— one of my best. I needed to run this one in order to qualify for the Boston Marathon, and I finished with a time of 3:09. Then I ran the Miami Half Marathon as training for the upcoming Boston race, where running through such knowledgeable and enthusiastic crowds was an amazing experience.

After that, I ran the New York City Marathon, racing through all five boroughs. It was like running through five different countries. As we were running over the Brooklyn Bridge, somebody yelled out, "What's going on?" Another person answered, "The bridge is bouncing!" It's the most weight that the bridge holds over the entire year. Hearing the roar of the crowd once we entered Fifth Avenue was quite a rush.

Next, I ran the Vermont City Marathon in Burlington. It was unusually warm for Vermont. That same year, I ran the Chicago Marathon, which ended up being my best time, 3:05. The following year, I ran the Chicago Marathon once more. When we passed the temperature gauge, it was already ninety-four degrees. We were able to finish, but the infamous race was stopped after three and a half hours. My final marathon was in beautiful Napa Valley.

Throughout all these races, I learned a tremendous amount. The races themselves were helpful in terms of my focus on training. For most of the races, I was able to do negative splits, running the second half of the race faster than the first. Even though at marathons the energy is incredibly heightened, I tried not to let it overpower or sway my race plan: first, to finish the race; second, to enjoy the race; and third, to make good time. Many people who came to cheer me on had never been to a race before. In many of the cities, I was interviewed by the local media. People seemed fascinated by a marathon-running Tibetan lama.

In all these races, I ran for a charitable cause, so it felt important to finish each race. Once I got into consistently good shape, I really wanted to run a three-hour marathon. However, the general purpose of these races was for a larger cause.

When you show up at a marathon, the universality of running is clearly evident in the diversity of the runners—people of all ages, shapes, and sizes. Dedication, joy, and pain binds us all. For being such an individual sport, running generates a powerful synergy.

FREEDOM
by Sakyong Mipham

Tantalizing, trepidatious,
I move one foot in front of the other.
I am a runner—
There is no greater joy in the three worlds.
When lightning strikes the earth,
That is the cosmic step taking place,
When my heart and lungs are placed in my hands.
Life is dependent on breathing and feeling.

What electricity comes forth
In the sweat I feel in my mouth,
Inspiration that allows me to traverse
Disbelief, laziness, daydreaming.
When I breathe, all of those windfalls
Pass by as billowing clouds
Seen by a boat set sail across the waters
Of confusion, summer, and time.

Within this temporal journey details are important.
I taste the sweet smell of water with its eight qualities,
Respecting this gift for my human body.
I revel in having time and space to run among the gods.
When I run I become one of those gods with no bounds—
Pure joy is my water bottle.

I am sustained with the ultimate elixir, my goo-ru.*
That vital inspiration sends me across this entire planet
With the pitter-patter of drala feet.

What bhumi can I not reach?
Placing my feet on the path, ripples affect the universe.
Therefore when I breathe,
I inhale all that is confused, degenerated, and unhappy.
When I exhale, my knee strikes high,
My Achilles is powerful, free from vulnerability.
Thus with the energy of surprise
I leap into this new dimension, which can only be seen
By the rapid movement of heart, feet, and mind.
May this incredible experience of movement
Be the source of all happiness.

SINGAPORE, 2005

---

* "Goo" is the high-carbohydrate gel that runners consume to sustain
their energy.

Acknowledgments

I would like to acknowledge many who have accompanied me on my path, my journey of running. For their cheerfulness, support, and friendship: Tarah (Misty) Cech, Jon Pratt, Eric Cech, Nick Trautz, Barry Gruessner, and Mike Sandrock. For accompanying me on many wonderful runs: Kyle Schaffhauser, Ben Medrano, Justin Robbins, Josh Silberstein, Mark Whaley, Christoph Schönherr, James Thorpe, Greg Wolk, Sean Raggett, Ralph Moosbrugger, Michael Fraund, Amy Conway, Glenn Austin, and Alan Goldstein. For their bodywork: Craig Mollins, Jim Asher, Jim Pascucci, Wells Christie, Tom Pathe, Ron Thompson, Mariah Simonton, Elaine Wong, and Peter Goodman. For their care: Dr. Mitchell Levy and Dr. Aaron Snyder. For their generosity: Michael and Jeanine Greenleaf, Nicolette de Hoop, Koos de Boer, and Radhe Shyam Saraf. For their support: H. E. Namkha Drimed Rinpoche and the Ripa family. For their service: the Dorje Kasung and the Dorje Kusung.

Thanks also to Emily Hilburn Sell for her constant encouragement and support, and to Reid Boates for his enthusiasm.

About the Author

||||||||||||||||||||||||||||||||||||||

Sakyong Mipham is the leader of Shambhala, a worldwide community of meditation retreat centers grounded in realizing basic goodness and enlightened society through daily life. He is also an avid runner who has completed nine marathons. *Planet* magazine has called him a "global visionary." He is the author of the bestselling *Turning the Mind into an Ally* and the award-winning *Ruling Your World*. Sakyong Mipham teaches all over the world, using his unique blend of Eastern and Western perspectives to the benefit of his students in North and South America, Europe, and Asia.

For current news about and teachings from Sakyong Mipham, see www.sakyong.com.

For more information about *Running with the Mind of Meditation,* see www.runningmind.org.

For more information about the Shambhala tradition of warriorship, see www.shambhala.org.